Women's Two Roles

Women's Two Roles

A Contemporary Dilemma

Phyllis Moen

Auburn House

New York • Westport, Connecticut • London

Library of Congress Cataloging-in-Publication Data

Moen, Phyllis.
    Women's two roles : a contemporary dilemma / Phyllis Moen.
      p. cm.
    Includes bibliographical references and index.
    ISBN 0–86569–198–3 (hc : alk. paper).—ISBN 0–86569–199–1 (pbk.)
      1. Working mothers—United States. 2. Mothers—Employment—United
States. 3. Work and family—United States. I. Title.
HQ759.48.M64 1992
305.42—dc20   91–36728

British Library Cataloguing in Publication Data is available.

Library of Congress Catalog Card Number: 91–36728
ISBN: 0–86569–198–3 (hc)
    0–86569–199–1 (pbk.)

First published in 1992

Auburn House, 88 Post Road West, Westport, CT 06881
An imprint of Greenwood Publishing Group, Inc.

Printed in the United States of America

The paper used in this book complies with the
Permanent Paper Standard issued by the National
Information Standards Organization (Z39.48–1984).

10 9 8 7 6 5 4 3 2

To Deborah and Melanie

CONTENTS

FIGURES

ACKNOWLEDGMENTS

Alva Myrdal and Viola Klein's classic book *Women's Two Roles: Home and Work* was published in Great Britain in 1956, at the height of the baby boom in the United States. The authors sought to present strategies that would enable women to combine their traditional family obligations with paid work. Today, although we recognize that women have many more than two roles, the work/family interface still poses a dilemma, and Myrdal and Klein's "sequencing" solution is, for most women, now out of date. Their book inspired me to take a new look at women, work, and family and to seek contemporary answers to a problem that has grown exponentially since the first *Women's Two Roles* was written. My goal was to examine long-term trends in American women's experiences and in their shifting societal contexts following World War II until the present, and to suggest how these trends shape future options.

In the pages that follow I describe the meshing of work and family roles not only as the private dilemmas of individual women and their families but also as a public dilemma for the nation. This is an issue linked to deep apprehensions about families' and children's well-being, to demands for gender equality, to the outcry of some for a return to the traditional wife-as-homemaker role, and to growing concerns about labor market needs, workers' productivity, and economic competitiveness. As such it is now very much on the contemporary American agenda.

I am deeply indebted to the people who offered assistance and encouragement in the writing of this book. Foremost is my husband Dick Shore, who provided intellectual and editorial collaboration as well as sustaining confidence. And second is John Modell, whose insights and assurances were always forthcoming. Roberta Balstad Miller of the National Science Foundation furnished the essential windows of time needed to complete the first draft while I was there as the Program Director of Sociology. Richard Rockwell and the Social Science Research Council supplied tangible assistance in getting the book off the ground. Melanie Lynn Moen, Kirstin Condry, and Irene Pytcher worked and reworked the data, figures, and bibliography; Roberta Maguire provided editorial assistance. Leeann Borden, Gina Bisagni, and Amy Honeck spent hours at the library. Alicia S. Merritt was an excellent editor. My colleagues at Cornell—Urie Bronfenbrenner, Joan Jacobs Brumberg, Donna Dempster-McClain, Henry Ricciuti, and Elaine Wethington— gave useful advice, as did the anonymous reviewers. Janet Kelly Moen, Dikkie Schoggen, and Carla B. Howery provided emotional support. And two generations of women in my life, my mother and her sisters—Etta Elkins, Evelyn Fairbanks, Jerry Elkins, Myrna Evans, and Peggy Whitley—my daughters and step-daughters—Deborah Moen Frickstad and Melanie Lynn Moen, Roberta Maguire and Linda Shore—have taught me firsthand about the dilemmas inherent in women's lives.

I   The Issue in Context

1 INTRODUCTION

> At this juncture in our social history women are guided by two apparently conflicting aims. On the one hand, they want, like everybody else, to develop their personalities to the full and to take an active part in adult social and economic life. . . . On the other hand, most women want a home and a family of their own.
>
> *(Myrdal and Klein 1956:xii)*

We in the United States are experiencing a radical transformation in the nature and character of family, work, and society itself, as mothers of young children enter and remain in the labor force in unprecedented numbers. What has changed so dramatically is *not* women's roles but their duration and sequence. Today a majority of American women engage in employment and child rearing *simultaneously*, a seemingly impossible feat in a world fashioned for families in which fathers serve as breadwinners and mothers as homemakers. And, as we shall see, because of the complex and unequal pace of social change, there are built-in contradictions and inconsistencies in what men and women raising families expect of themselves and each other, in what employers expect of workers, and in what society expects of its male and female members.

Throughout history women have been workers as well as wives and mothers—but not necessarily at the *same time*. In the aftermath of the Industrial Revolution, marked by the separation of paid work from home life, women held work and family roles *sequentially*.[1] Young unmarried girls commonly worked in factories or as domestics. When they married they left their jobs if it were financially possible to do so. As wives and mothers, women also contributed to the family economy when necessary, but at times and in ways that did not seriously conflict with their principal homemaking responsibilities—by doing piecework at home, washing other people's laundry, or taking in boarders.[2] For most women, sequencing work and family roles meant working outside the home before marriage and motherhood, and then permanently withdrawing from the labor force in order to tend to household and child-care obligations.

The first half of the twentieth century added another form of sequencing, as women gradually began returning to employment after their children were grown. In fact, by 1945 the "average" female worker in the United States was married and over 35.

In the mid-1950s, Alva Myrdal and Viola Klein's book on women's two roles argued that women could successfully mesh their home and work roles and need not "forgo the pleasures of one sphere in order to enjoy the satisfactions of the other" (1956:xiii). The optimal arrangement, as they saw it, was precisely through role sequencing, with family and work roles each "given its own place in a chronological sequence" (p. 155). Their proposed solution was for women to continue the practice of leaving the labor force to bear and raise children but to reenter it earlier, as soon as their children reached school age.

From the 1950s on, women in fact have spent increasingly larger portions of their adulthood in employment, typically in the sequential fashion recommended by Myrdal and Klein. But unlike earlier generations, American mothers in the 1970s, 1980s, and now in the 1990s have returned to employment even more quickly—or have never even left it. By 1990 over half (59.4%) of the married mothers of preschoolers and, even more strikingly, over half (51.3%) of the mothers of infants (children under age one) were in the labor force.

We in the United States stand at something of a crossroads. A shrinking labor force, the rising costs of living, and notions of gender equality render women's employment ever more essential and desirable, but customary institutional patterns (at home and at work) make combining the mothering of young children with employment both frustrating and exhausting, if not impossible. There are no blueprints for where we go from here.

This book provides a contemporary view of trends in women's work and family roles in the United States. To be sure, women enact many roles—daughter, sister, friend, volunteer, and neighbor, to name a few—but it is the wife/mother family role that is central to most women's identity, and it is the employment role that has become increasingly prominent in women's lives, as it has always been in men's. It is the *combination* of employment with the mothering of babies and toddlers that is especially demanding—and controversial. Women's changing roles are now being widely and often emotionally discussed and debated in the media, in the classroom, and in government, as well as at work and at home. This is by no means a new issue; social scientists have studied and written about women's employment throughout much of the twentieth century. What *is* new, however, is the urgency with which these discussions and debates are voiced, as working mothers of infants and preschoolers become an established fact of life. Social observers have concluded that women's lives will never again resemble what we think of as traditional, and this transformation penetrates to the heart of two of our most fundamental institutions: the family and the economy.

The book's organizing theme underscores the unevenness and complexity of this social change, both for American society in general and for individuals and their families. Ambivalence, uneasiness, and recalcitrance pervade social attitudes, actions, and institutional arrangements and encompass several separate but intertwined realities.

The first reality is that we are experiencing a *transition in progress*. This means that there is considerable diversity in the ways in which American women organize their lives. It also means that frequently there is a discrepancy between women's actual behavior and their own personal preferences. Some employed mothers feel full of conflict about their work or feel as though they are captives of their jobs, wishing they were instead full-time homemakers. Conversely, some homemakers see themselves as captives, wanting to work outside the home but lacking the education, job skills, or child-care arrangements to make employment economically or logistically feasible. Still other women have resolved work/family cross-pressures by accommodating one to the other, perhaps by having fewer children or by working only part-time. But growing numbers are strongly committed to their jobs and are reluctant to forego career opportunities for family obligations.

This transition in progress introduces the notion of cohort replacement, with social change occurring as younger people replace older ones, over time, within society. Consider the panoply of changes in virtually every aspect of women's lives and how these are disproportionately experienced by younger women. In contrast to their mothers or grandmothers, American women now in their 20s and 30s are better educated, have fewer children, and bear them later in life. They are postponing marriage and are less likely to marry or to stay married. And they are more likely than ever to be employed, regardless of their family responsibilities. Decisions about marriage and divorce, the number and timing of children, and personal aspirations all influence and are influenced by whether or not women are employed. As younger cohorts replace older ones over time, new life-styles may emerge—for men as well as for women.

A second reality concerns *deeply entrenched ideologies* in the United States about families, individuals, and government. We have long upheld a "doctrine of two spheres," which designates the home and family as a private arena, the place where children should be taught values and belief systems, and very much the special province of wives and mothers. The sanctity of the family means that it has been put off limits to government intrusion. Moreover, the traditional emphasis in the United States on free enterprise and on the supremacy of the individual, along with the pluralistic nature of our society, has long precluded the adoption of family goals on the political agenda. The laissez-faire orientation of our society has underscored the preeminence of economic interests, as illustrated by President Bush's 1990 veto of the Family and Medical Leave Act, which established government mandates presumed injurious to the business community. An emphasis on individualism militates against government intervention into family life and often gives birth to policies that are antithetical to the best interests of families and children.

Regional, ethnic, and religious differences in values have precluded a consensus on the meaning of family well-being, much less a common understanding of the "proper" roles of women and men within society. Similarly, the layered structure of government—city, county, state, federal, as well as executive, legislative, and judicial—encourages a patchwork of often incompatible legislation and regulation in lieu of a national policy that addresses the quandaries growing out of maternal employment.

We in the United States confront a true cultural dilemma, with the employment of mothers at odds with ingrained values concerning the family. While Americans of all ages increasingly endorse the notion of *wives'* employment, many remain uneasy about the employment of *mothers of young children*. There are inherent cultural contradictions in having mothers of young children employed, since women still have the principal responsibility for child care. Although the federal government is noticeably reluctant to intervene in providing supports for working mothers (or parents), it seeks to promote women's equality of opportunity. American society thus conveys a mixed message, one which reinforces the primacy of domesticity in women's lives but also stresses the increasing significance of their employment.[3]

And finally, there is the third reality of *structural lags*, a mismatch between prevailing institutional conditions and the spiraling numbers of mothers in the work force. We have traditionally operated on the premise that wives and mothers would do the domestic labor of society in order to free husbands and fathers to work in the paid economy. Now that these wives and mothers are themselves workers, new social arrangements are needed. The fact that almost half the labor force is now female challenges well-entrenched employment policies and practices designed for an essentially male work force, a work force without child-care responsibilities. But like all other institutions, the world of work is resistant to change. New and more appropriate policies and practices will come about only when the economic and social costs of doing nothing outweigh the costs of change.

A variant of the "structural lag" reality introduces the concept of patriarchy: Since men benefit from traditional domestic and workplace arrangements of their making, they are reluctant to see them altered.

These three realities—a transition in progress, ideological traditions, and structural lags—point up both similarities and differences between the United States and other advanced societies. European nations are also in a transitional phase and are experiencing major shifts in gender roles and in the configuration of families (Sorrentino 1990). Thus, the United States is not alone in facing the dilemma of women's two roles. However, this country *is* unique in its reluctance to join the issue in the policy arena. European countries, unlike the United States, provide supports to women, parents, and families in the form of children's allowances, maternity benefits, and paid parental leaves of absence. These supports reflect both convictions about the importance of families and children's welfare and pragmatic concerns about low birthrates and, consequently, a diminishing labor force.[4]

By contrast, the United States, while paying lip service to the importance of families and children, gives an even higher regard to the ethic of individualism and the tenets of the free enterprise system and has been notably reluctant to pay the costs of significantly expanded government benefits and services for women, for working parents, or for families.

The roles of men and women are undergoing a progressive transformation in all advanced societies, but the rate of change among them varies considerably. Sweden, for example, has taken the lead in fashioning structural mechanisms to promote a reconciliation of work and family roles, for both men and women (Moen 1989). Still, citizens in some European countries, such as Germany and Great Britain, express an ambivalence similar to that voiced in the United States about the employment of mothers of young children (Alwin, Braun, and Scott 1990). And even in Sweden it is women who continue to have the primary responsibility for home and family.

We in the United States, individually and collectively, remain uncertain, if not divided, as to what men's and women's roles should be. Prevailing attitudes here about women, maternal employment, children, and families remain ambivalent and contradictory. This is of pivotal importance in seeking to understand the absence of any coherent political or private sector response to the changing work/family relationship in this country. Because of the absence of any consensus about women's roles, or of the role of government in family matters, we are markedly reluctant to adopt social policies and institutional arrangements designed to reduce the inevitable conflicts and overloads of combining employment with family responsibilities, despite the fact that currently over half of American mothers of preschoolers are employed.

The following chapter details the trends in women's labor force participation in the United States, focusing especially on the dramatic influx of mothers of young children into the work force. It also charts shifts in social attitudes about women's roles as well as a spectrum of other, demographic, alterations.

Chapter 3 describes the various strategies American women have used to balance home and work obligations, and it evaluates the impact of employment on their well-being. It asks whether paid work is beneficial or detrimental to women's mental and physical health.

Chapter 4 examines the implications of maternal employment for families. How has the growing number of employed mothers of young children influenced the household division of labor between husbands and wives? The marital relationship? Has it affected the well-being of men? Of children? This social revolution has transformed not only women's lives; men are more likely than ever before to be married to working wives, and most children now have working mothers. What are the short- and long-term consequences for children of growing up in homes where mothers, as well as fathers, are in the labor force?

Chapter 5 presents major work force trends and documents the changing demography of the world of work. Population and economic forecasts suggest that women increasingly will be needed in the labor force in the years ahead in order to sustain our economic growth and preserve our present standard of living. In this light, what have been the responses to maternal employment of three key institutions: government, business, and labor unions?

Chapter 6 concludes that the "problem" of maternal employment is not going to disappear of its own accord. We have, at least theoretically, a number of options open to us. At one end of the spectrum is a return to traditional family roles; at the other, is the adoption by women of the male model of continuous employment over the life course. We can, nevertheless, infer from the evidence at hand that (1) most women in the United States will have children and most will be employed while raising their children and (2) families with infants and toddlers and two full-time breadwinners (or one full-time single-parent breadwinner) face considerable time pressure, overload, and strain.

The challenge is not for women to become exactly like men in their work lives, or to return to the domestic hearth, but for us as a nation to restructure *both* family and work roles, for *both* men and women. Part of the problem is how the life course is organized in our society. We march lock step from schooling to work to retirement, which means that the work years coincide, unfortunately, with the childbearing years. This makes successfully combining working with parenting difficult, if not impossible, for women, when "working" means forty or more hours per week on the job and "parenting" means women having full-time and almost exclusive responsibility for their children. We need to redesign the way in which we live—moving away from the fixed sequence of education in the early years, employment during most of adulthood, and leisure (in the form of retirement) in the later years—to introduce greater diversity and flexibility. Alternative life pathways could include a period of reduced work hours or even sabbaticals for fathers and/or mothers while their children are infants and toddlers, with no loss of seniority or job security.

In this book I argue that we as a society are managing only because of the makeshift accommodations of individual women and their families. But everyone suffers as a consequence: Women with young children are exhausted, family life is hectic, the workplace is often disrupted, and work at home and work on the job continue to be defined and limited by gender. We must adopt, as a matter of national policy, basic *structural* changes in our institutions—modifying the time and timing of employment and providing available, affordable, and quality child care. These changes, along with more flexible life pathways, can substantially reduce the personal strains and the career costs borne so disproportionately by women. But they also can provide men as well as women with greater latitude in shaping their lives and in raising their families. Equally important, these structural changes can engender a more stable and productive work force in an era when economic growth depends heavily on our human resources. The coupling of work and family roles is a major challenge that we, as a nation, have only begun to address, one that stands to be even more formidable in the coming years.

NOTES

1. In the early phases of the Industrial Revolution women were not excluded from employment. However, a combination of forces culminated in their relegation to the domestic sphere. See the discussions by Hartmann (1976), Walby (1986), Cohn (1985), and Tentler (1979). Throughout this book I use the words "working" and "employed" interchangeably, as is common usage; however, I am nonetheless cognizant of the fact that homemakers indeed work, although they are not paid for their labor. Here, however, I am concentrating on *paid labor force participation*.

2. A number of historians have written about this subject (Banner 1974; Degler 1980; Evans 1989; Katzman 1977; Mintz and Kellogg 1988; Modell and Hareven 1973; Tilly and Scott 1978).

3. For a discussion of the doctrine of two spheres, see Cott and Pleck (1979) and Degler (1980). A fuller discussion of the ambivalence concerning policies affecting family life is found in Moen and Schorr (1987) and Klatch (1987). An important ingredient in the drive toward equality of employment opportunity for women was the Civil Rights Act of 1964. An example of societal ambivalence about maternal employment is seen in the Family Support Act of 1988, which requires certain mothers receiving welfare Aid to Families with Dependent Children (AFDC) to enroll in work programs.

4. European countries, unlike the United States, have had strict immigration policies and therefore rely on their own citizens to meet labor force demands. Thus their investment in policies conducive to fertility and to the quality of the next generation relate not only to family well-being but also to the labor market (Kamerman, Kahn, and Kingston 1983; Kamerman and Kahn 1988; Gladstone, Williams, and Belous 1985; Moen 1989).

2   RECENT TRENDS

The people who live the trends that government statisticians count
have had to discard traditional expectations without yet establishing
new ones.

(Strasser 1982:304)

PATTERNS OF WOMEN'S LABOR FORCE ATTACHMENT

The increasing labor force participation of women has been a long-term
trend throughout this century. In 1900, one in five American women was
employed in paid work, a proportion that rose gradually to over one in
four by 1940.[1]

But World War II marked a pivotal point in women's labor force
attachment. Not only did the *proportion* of women increase (from 27%
in 1940 to 35% in 1944), but the *composition* of the female segment of
the labor force also changed markedly. Prior to the war most employed
women were either single, holding jobs until they married, or wives from
low-income, often black or immigrant families, who typically contributed to the family economy by performing domestic services in other
homes. During the war years, however, middle-class housewives began
entering the labor force in record numbers, especially those whose
children no longer required full-time care.[2]

The proportion of wives in the labor force increased by half from 1940
to 1944 (from 14.7% to 21.7%), marking the beginning of a remarkable
reorganization of women's life patterns (see Figure 2.1). In fact, 75
percent of the new female entrants during the war were wives. For the

Figure 2.1
Trends in Women's Participation in the Labor Force, 1900–1990

Sources: U.S. Bureau of the Census 1975b: 133; 1990b: 384; Hayghe 1991.
Note: Data 1900–1930 from decennial census refer to civilian population (including
institutional) 15 years and over. Data 1940–1965 refer to civilian population 14
years and over.

first time in history over half of the female labor force in the United
States was married; by 1945 the majority of women workers were over
age 35.

Surprisingly, there was no mass exodus back to the kitchen at the war's
end. To be sure, there was a brief turnaround; women's labor force
participation rate fell 5 percentage points from 1944 to 1947 (from 35%
to 30%). But after the war married women continued to move into
employment, especially those in midlife (ages 45–59) whose years of
child rearing were ending.

Still, these changes in women's employment during and following
World War II did not significantly alter the primacy of women's family
role. The family work—of child care, husband care, housework, and
emotional "work"—still preoccupied and restricted women's lives.
Most women reentered the labor force only after their children were
in school or had been launched from the home. So long as their children
were young, women's principal functions continued to be caretakers
and homemakers. This created a "dip" in women's labor force participation during the early adult years, when wives took time out for

homemaking and child care. However, even this dip soon began to disappear.[3]

Social change is reflected in individual lives in two ways: (1) People of all ages can modify their attitudes or behavior (individual change), and (2) younger birth cohorts can adopt new orientations or life-styles, with society changing as these cohorts grow older, replacing those who preceded them (cohort replacement). Both types of change have produced the transformation of women's roles. Although women of all ages have returned to the labor force, even more important, each succeeding birth cohort has developed a progressively stronger attachment to employment.

For example, women born during the depression years of 1931–35 typically left work when they were in their late 20s; but, by their late 30s and early 40s, half of them held jobs once again. Women born during the war years (1941-45) also left their jobs during their late 20s, but they returned to paid work even earlier; fully 55 percent had resumed employment by their early 30s. And most women born in the 1950s and later have left their jobs only for short periods of time, if at all, when they have children.

By 1980 the dip in women's labor force participation during the childbearing stage had disappeared. This was a landmark year. Not only were over half of all American women in the labor force in 1980, but, for the first time, half of all *wives* were employed outside the home, a proportion that had increased to 58.4 percent by 1990.[4]

Shifts in the median age of women workers mirror these life-cycle transformations in women's employment. In 1900 half of all employed women were under 26 years of age, reflecting the relative youth of single women workers at the turn of the century. By 1970 the median age had risen to 38 years, marking the movement of wives in midlife into employment throughout the 1960s. This average age dropped to 34 years in 1980, as younger wives and mothers remained in the labor force despite their family obligations.[5]

The number of working wives more than tripled from 1950 to 1990, increasing from 8 million to over 29 million. This represents a remarkable transformation of the traditional wife/mother/homemaker role, and it occurred across race and ethnic groups. Over half (54.6%) of the wives of Hispanic origin were in the labor force in 1989; even larger proportions of white (57.0%) and black wives (65.7%) were working. In fact, race and ethnicity are increasingly less salient in predicting women's employment.[6]

Maternal Employment

Over 19 million mothers are now in the labor force, representing more than six out of every ten women with children under 18 years of age. This fact becomes particularly impressive when it is viewed against the backdrop of the past. In 1950 only 18 percent of mothers with children under 18 were in the labor force; by 1990 this had more than tripled to 63 percent.

Even more striking has been the growth in the employment of mothers of preschool children. In 1950, only 12 percent of wives and mothers of preschoolers were employed; by 1990 this had escalated to 59.4 percent, an almost fivefold increase. This unprecedented shift occurred across the board, regardless of marital status or race. In fact, the most noteworthy trend throughout the 1970s and 1980s was the escalating proportion of *married* mothers of preschoolers with jobs—rising over 25 percentage points from 1970 to 1990 (see Figure 2.2). Although divorced mothers are still more likely to work outside the home, marital status, like race, has become less consequential in distinguishing between mothers who are employed and those who are full-time homemakers.

Figure 2.2
Trends in Mothers of Preschoolers in the Labor Force, by Marital Status, 1950–1988

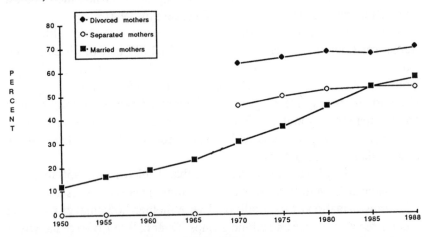

Source: U.S. Bureau of the Census 1990b: 385.
Note: Preschoolers are defined as children under age 6.

Mothers of Infants

Having a young child—even an infant—is no longer a major deterrent to women's employment. By 1990 over half the mothers with infants under 12 months of age were in the labor force, as were three out of every five mothers of 2-year-old toddlers (see Figure 2.3).

This was arguably the most distinctive alteration that took place in women's lives in the 1980s. The largest change occurred among white women. In 1976 the labor force participation rate of white women who gave birth the past year was 28.6 percent, a proportion which grew to 49.4 by 1988, representing an increase of 72 percent. For black mothers of infants, the labor force participation rate rose from 43.2 percent in 1976 to 58.6 by 1988, an increase of 36 percent. Although no data are available on Hispanic mothers of infants in 1976, by 1988 the labor force participation rate for this group was 36.6 percent.[7]

An examination of trends from 1976 to 1985 in the labor force participation of mothers of newborns reveals that the largest increase occurred among mothers who were between 30 and 40 years of age,

Figure 2.3
Trends in Wives with Infants and Toddlers in the Labor Force, 1970–1988

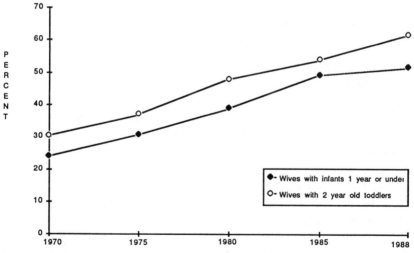

Sources: Waldman 1983; U.S. Bureau of the Census 1990: 385.
Note: Data as of March of each year.

white, and not currently married, who had at least some college. Three types of women were most likely to return to work before their infants were a year old:

1. *The Young Mother*. This is the young (under age 24) married mother, with only a high school education, who has given birth to her first child. In 1976 there was only one chance in three (34%) of her returning to work while her child was an infant; in 1985 the odds were greater than one in two (54%).
2. *The Delayed Childbearer*. This woman has completed at least some college and has postponed starting her family until after age 24. The odds of her returning to work before the child's first birthday were over two in five in 1976 (44%) but more than three in five (64%) in 1985.
3. *The Unmarried Mother*. This woman is a white high school graduate who already has two or more children and has been married but is now either divorced or separated. The likelihood of her being in the labor force while her infant is under 12 months of age doubled from 1976 to 1985 (from 27% to 54%). By contrast, the probability that the young (18 to 24), black, never married mother who has not finished high school will quickly return to employment *declined* slightly during these years from 34 to 31 percent.[8]

TRENDS IN PUBLIC ATTITUDES TOWARD GENDER ROLES

The picture is complicated because women, who are themselves changing, have to be viewed against a moving historical backdrop. (Giele 1982:143)

In the early part of this century people saw the employment of wives and mothers as a "temporary expedient in hard times" (Tentler 1979:141). By the standard of that period, the successful family was one that could afford to have a wife who was a full-time homemaker.

This orientation was especially pronounced during the Great Depression of the 1930s, reinforced by the concern that wives were or would be taking jobs away from men. In fact, during this era twenty-six states enacted laws *prohibiting* the hiring of married women. A national poll conducted in 1938 revealed a widespread consensus regarding men's and women's roles. Over four-fifths (82%) of the men and three-fourths (75%) of the women surveyed believed that wives should not work if their husbands were employed. When such questions were again asked in 1972, a majority of the men (63%) and women (68%) had come to endorse wives' employment. By 1976 still larger proportions (65% of men and 70% of women) expressed approval "of a married woman earning money in business or industry if she has a husband capable of supporting her." What happened? Did changes in attitudes *cause* or did they *follow* changes in women's labor force behavior?[9]

Historians and other social observers generally pinpoint World War II, with its civilian labor shortage, as the period when first women's behavior and then social attitudes changed. According to William Chafe,

If the nation—including women—had been asked in 1939 whether it desired, or would tolerate such a far-reaching change, the answer would undoubtedly have been an overwhelming no. But events bypassed public opinion, and made the change an accomplished fact. The war, in short, was a catalyst which broke up old modes of behavior and helped to forge new ones. (1972:247)

To be sure, war work became synonymous with patriotism, and womanpower became pivotal to winning the war. Opinion polls conducted in 1942 reveal that 60 percent of those surveyed agreed that married women should work in war industries. The War Department, as well as the War Manpower Commission, launched propaganda campaigns to recruit housewives into the labor force. For example, the Office of War Information challenged married women by asking, "Are you being old-fashioned and getting by just being a 'good wife and mother'?" (Margolis 1984:215).

But some researchers underscore the complexity of this societal change, arguing that the war "did not make a drastic break with traditional working patterns or sex roles" (Campbell 1984: 85). To be sure, the war was a watershed in married women's labor force behavior, but home and family remained women's preoccupation. By the 1950s wives were again encouraged to be homemakers on a full-time basis. As Agnes E. Mayer said in a 1950 *Atlantic Monthly* article, "Women have many careers but only one vocation—motherhood" (quoted in Evans 1989:245). In fact, many women went to work in the 1950s *because* of their families, to improve their standard of living. Following the war, women found themselves caught between "the promise of change and the restoration of tradition" (Berkin and Lovett 1980:3).

Still, the postwar period marked a dramatic reversal in public objections to married women's employment.[10] Recall that two kinds of social changes could have been taking place: (1) changes *across* cohorts, as young people with more liberal orientations became adults and replaced older, more conservative adults (cohort replacement) and (2) individual changes *within* cohorts, as people of all ages adopted attitudes about wives' employment more in harmony with the values of an increasingly egalitarian society (individual change). Whether the shifts in the acceptance of wives' employment have been principally a consequence of individual changes in attitudes or cohort replacement can be determined by examining age differences over time. Survey data suggest that both factors have propelled the change. Younger cohorts are more liberal in their attitudes, but older cohorts also have changed their opinions regarding married women's employment over the years.[11]

These trends continued throughout the 1980s. From 1977 to 1985 men of all educational levels became more egalitarian in their outlook about women's employment; only women college graduates—already typically egalitarian—experienced little change in gender-role attitudes.

But the liberalization of sex-role attitudes over the past thirty years did not occur uniformly. Rather, whites began to catch up with blacks in egalitarian views as did men with women. And women with less education became more like college graduates in their gender-role orientations. Men too became more supportive of women working, but they were less enthusiastic about the employment of mothers of young children. Still, appreciable shifts unfolded among men and women of all ages; the liberalization of gender-role ideology has not been the exclusive province of the young.[12]

Why do individuals change their minds about whether married women should engage in paid work? In part, at least, their education and their experiences (or those of their wives or mothers) affect their attitudes. One study traced a group of Detroit women who were first interviewed as new mothers in 1962 and reinterviewed in 1977 and 1980, at which time their children were also interviewed (Thornton and Freedman 1979; Thornton, Alwin, and Camburn 1983). Women who returned to school or who spent more years in paid work, as well as those with more educated husbands, were especially apt to change their views about women's roles. Moreover, their 18–year-old daughters were consistently less traditional in 1980 than their mothers had been in 1962. However, traditionally oriented mothers tended to have more traditionally oriented sons and daughters, suggesting some transfer of gender-role attitudes across the generations.

This societal trend in the growing acceptance in the United States of the employment of married women is reflected in shifts in the decisions and life plans of individual women. For example, a 1943 survey of sophomores in an Eastern women's college revealed that three out of five (61%) planned not to work after marriage. By contrast, in a 1979 survey of freshman at the same college, only five percent planned to concentrate exclusively on home and family and nearly half (48%) intended to combine careers and family life with a minimal interlude for childbearing, a goal that few (12%) had expressed in 1943. The data from these small samples of students in 1943 and 1979 capture in a modest way the enormous change in the options envisioned by young women. This acceptance of women meshing employment and family life is reaffirmed in the findings of national surveys polling college freshmen from 1967 through 1988 (see Figure 2.4). In 1967 two-thirds of the young men entering college agreed that "the activities of married women are best confined to the home and family," but by 1988, fewer than one-third (32%) of male college freshmen endorsed this statement. For freshmen women the proportions agreeing with the statement dropped from 44 percent in 1967 to 20 percent in 1988. These surveys illustrate the apparent convergence between men's and women's attitudes about married women's employment; the 22 percent difference between the sexes in 1967 had fallen to 12 percent by 1988.

Figure 2.4
Trends in College Freshmen Agreeing with the Premise, "The Activities of Married Women Are Best Confined to the Home and Family," 1967–1988

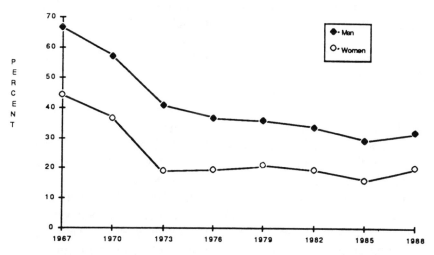

Sources: Astin, Green, and Korn, 1987: 50, 74; Astin, Green, Korn, Schalit, and Berz 1989: 29, 45.

Attitudes about Maternal Employment

It is one thing to accept the employment of married women generally but quite another to endorse the employment of mothers of young children. Unfortunately, questions about maternal employment were not asked in opinion surveys until 1970. In that year a study of gender-role attitudes among a national sample of never married women under age 45 found that concern about the potentially harmful effects of maternal employment on preschool children was closely related to the acceptance of traditional role distinctions. Those who felt that "a preschool child is likely to suffer if his mother works" tended to agree that "it is much better for everyone involved if the man is the achiever outside the home and the woman takes care of home and family" (Mason and Bumpass 1975). By 1977 fully six out of ten women and seven out of ten men still believed that "a preschool child is likely to suffer if his or her mother works." The proportions concerned that harm is done to preschoolers declined rapidly between 1977 and 1985, but over two-fifths (46.9%) of the women and three-fifths (62.7%) of the men surveyed in 1985 still agreed that preschoolers might indeed suffer from the employment of their mothers. Karen Mason and Yu-Hsia Lu (1988) suggest that men may find it more acceptable for *wives* to work than for *mothers* to do so, especially mothers of preschoolers. But women also are worried about the impact of maternal employment on children. Asked about which gets slighted the most when a woman has a job and is a wife and mother, about equal numbers of men and women in a national sample conducted in 1985 mention the children (46% and 43%, respectively). In another survey, conducted in 1989, roughly the same proportions (46% and 44%) again felt that children were slighted.[13]

What about the next generation, the men and women who are most likely to combine full-time employment with child rearing? We find no major cohort change in the concern about the harm of maternal employment for children; this concern, therefore, is not likely to disappear as younger, more liberal men and women replace their more conservative elders. Consider, for example, the attitudes of high school seniors. About three out of five males in 1980 and again in 1985 believed that a preschooler is likely to suffer if the mother works, even though a declining proportion agreed that women should take care of the family while the man is the achiever outside the home (see Figure 2.5). Moreover, the proportions of young women disturbed about the effects of employment on preschoolers remained fairly steady, even increasing slightly, from 1980 to 1985. These convictions are best viewed in the

Figure 2.5
Gender-Role Attitudes of High School Seniors, by Sex, 1980, 1985

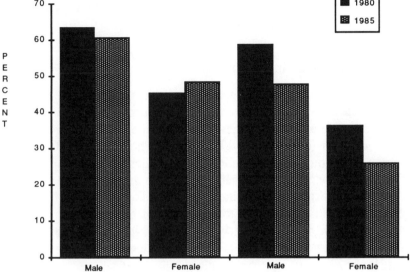

Sources: Herzog, Bachman and Johnson 1983; Johnston, Bachman, and O'Malley, 1986.
Note: Percent saying they agree or mostly agree.

context of broader changes in the orientations of women high school seniors. Although they consistently report marriage and family as extremely important life goals, growing numbers of women in high school also value income and opportunities for advancement (Johnston, Bachman, and O'Malley 1986). Relating these rising aspirations to their misgivings about the effects of maternal employment on young children may well herald role strains and conflicts for these young women in the years to come.

The disjuncture, for women as well as men, between an acceptance of gender equality and the belief that a mother's employment may harm her young children may reflect not so much an ambivalence about women's roles as a realistic appraisal of current options. Jobs are structured for individuals (typically males), not for workers with child-care responsibilities. And, as we shall see in Chapter 4, men continue to view domestic duties as the province mainly of their wives. Moreover, as documented in Chapter 5, only modest changes have occurred in the availability of child care, parental leaves of absence, reduced work schedules, or other supports for working parents. Beliefs about the deleterious effects of maternal employment on young children may say more about the lack of these supports for working parents than about whether mothers of young children should or should not work.

Linking Attitudes and Behavior

The dynamics of the connection between attitudes and behavior remain unclear.[14] Have women entered the labor force *because of* shifts in their sex-role attitudes, or have their attitudes changed as a *consequence of* their employment experience? The answers offered by research to this question are mixed. Some studies find that employment influences attitudes about women's roles, but they detect no effect in the opposite direction. Others find that sex-role orientations—including the husband's attitudes—do affect subsequent employment. The fact that employment has historically been discretionary for most wives suggests that their attitudes may well influence their labor force involvement. [15]

OTHER DEMOGRAPHIC AND SOCIAL TRANSFORMATIONS

Our society is engaged in rewriting the script for the role of women as mothers. (Bernard 1974:xiii)

The Women's Movement

We have seen that the 1970s decade in the United States was marked by a notable transformation of public attitudes toward women's roles. The majority of American men and women came to accept and even endorse the labor force participation of married women, and the traditional housewife role became even more devalued, despite the fact that by 1980 half of all married women still functioned as full-time homemakers (Andre 1981).

The 1970s also saw the flowering of the women's movement, encompassing a range of individuals, ideologies, and collective efforts aimed at promoting women's rights in all facets of society. This movement not only inspired legislation but gave legitimacy to women's quest for equality and engendered a new consciousness and self-concept among women. It, along with a variety of demographic, economic, and social transformations in the 1970s, resulted in more options open to American women than had been available to any previous generation. But many of the forces shaping women's lives and being shaped by women's choices are long-term trends—in fertility, educational attainment, marriage, female-headed families, wage rates, and poverty. These trends have profound implications for the labor force choices of mothers of infants and pre-schoolers in the 1990s and beyond. Women are caught up in a tide of change that makes paid work both more attractive and more financially essential, even while their children are young. By the 1990s for most American mothers *not being employed*, for any extended period of time, has become less of a realistic option.[16]

Trends in Fertility

Following the postwar baby boom—which lasted through the 1950s and into the 1960s—women expected to have ever smaller families. In 1967, wives aged 18 to 34 planned to have, on the average, 3.05 children; by 1988, wives in this age group planned for an average of only 2.22 children. This decline in anticipated births has characterized all races, although black and Hispanic women still plan on—and still have—larger families than do white women.

As more wives and mothers work outside the home, the number of children actually born per woman has in fact declined. During the peak of the baby boom era (1955–1959) the fertility rate averaged 3.69; by the mid-1980s (1985–1986) it dropped markedly to 1.84 children per woman (for differences by race see Figure 2.6), and it is projected by the Census Bureau to remain at about that level over the next twenty years.[17]

There also have been changes in the *timing* of childbearing. During the baby boom years of the 1950s a large proportion of women began their families when they were in their early 20s. In the 1960s more women delayed childbearing until their late 20s, and in the 1970s and 1980s many delayed childbearing until their 30s. In fact, the births per 1,000 women from 30 to 34 years of age increased by 45 percent from 1976 to 1988, and the number born to women 35 to 39 years of age was 50 percent higher in 1988 than in 1976.[18] Moreover, there has been a clear trend in the number of childless wives expecting a future birth. Among childless wives aged from 25 to 29, the percentage expecting a future birth increased from 75 percent in 1975 to 80 percent in 1988. For childless wives in the 30 to 34 age group, there was an even more dramatic increase: By 1988 54.4 percent expected a future birth, up from 34

Figure 2.6
Trends in Total Fertility Rate, 1940–1986

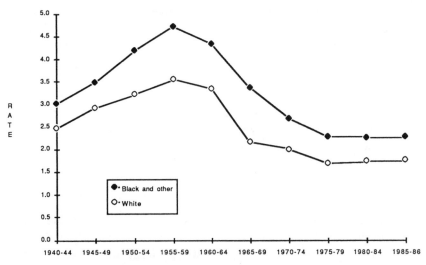

Source: U.S. Bureau of the Census 1990: 65.
Notes: Total fertility rate is the number of births that 1,000 women would have in
  their lifetime if, at each year of age, they experienced the birthrates occurring in
  the specified year (divided by 1,000).

  A rate of 2.11 represents "replacement level" fertility for the total population
  under current mortality conditions (assuming no net migration).

percent in 1975. These changes illustrate the kinds of social change
resulting from cohort replacement; younger cohorts of women, in
contrast to older ones, are reducing their fertility and are delaying their
childbearing in an unprecedented fashion. However, there was a 4 percent
jump in childbearing in 1990, including women in their 20s (Vobejda
1991). Since these mothers also have a history and expectation of work
force participation, a rise in fertility only means a rise in the work/family
dilemma.

   The average number of children remains about two, and small families
mean a firmer attachment to the labor force. Three-fourths of the mothers
with just one child were employed in 1987; only one-fourth of the
single-parent mothers and half the mothers in two parent families with
five or more children were employed. Also, delays in childbearing
promote labor force involvement. Over half (53.6%) of the women aged

from 30 to 44 with infants in 1988 were employed, compared to slightly less than half (49.4%) of those from 18 to 29 with infants.[19]

Trends in Educational Attainment

Women have made extraordinary educational gains over the last few decades. In 1960, only 35 percent of the young women who graduated from high school enrolled in college, compared to 46 percent of the young men; but, by 1986, over half (55% to 54%, respectively) of both groups were enrolling in college.

The proportion of higher degrees awarded to women has increased as well, and this has been a long-term trend throughout the century (see Figure 2.7). (The postwar dip reflects the influx of men into higher education, encouraged and assisted by the G.I. Bill's educational benefit provisions for war veterans.) A concurrent trend has been the decrease in racial differences in educational attainment, with black women "catching up" to white women in college completion (Farley 1984).

Education is closely related to employment: The more education a woman has, the more likely she is to be in the labor force. This education/employment relationship has intensified over time. Thus, in 1970 three out of five women with college degrees were in the labor force, compared to only a little over two out of five of those with less than a high school diploma. By 1988 the proportion of those with less than a high school degree in the labor force had not changed much, but by then over four out of five women with college degrees were in the labor force.[20]

These developments represent social change in the form of both cohort replacement (younger women are more likely to be better educated) and individual change (educated women of all ages are more likely to be employed). These two trends portend a still further escalation in women's interest in employment. Investing in education means, for most women, expanding career aspirations, and these aspirations compound the problem of combining work and family roles.

Trends in Marriage

Since the 1950s, growing numbers of young people have been either postponing marriage or choosing "singlehood" as a life-style. By 1989 the median age of first marriage for women had risen to 23.8 years and for men to 26.2 years. This contrasts with 20.3 years for women and 22.8 for men in the 1950s.[21]

Figure 2.7
Trends in Higher Education Degrees Awarded to Women, by Level of Degree, 1899–1901 to 1989–1990

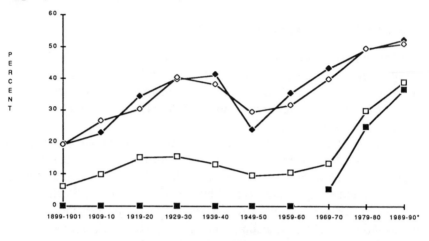

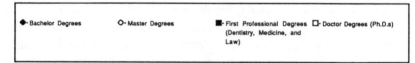

Source: U.S. Department of Education 1988: 189.
Note: First professional degrees are included with bachelor degrees prior to 1969–1970.
*Projected

These delays in the timing of marriage underlie the growing number of single young adults. In 1989 three out of every five women (62.5%) in their early 20s (20–24 years old) had never married, more than twice as many as in 1960 (28.4%). In the same age group, over three out of four (77.4%) men were never married in 1989, compared to over half (53.1%) in 1960.

Even more striking are marriage trends in the 25–29 age group; the proportion of never married women almost tripled (from 10.5% in 1960 to 29.4% in 1989), and the proportion of never married men more than doubled (from 20.8% in 1960 to 45.9% in 1989). The racial contrasts are noteworthy: Over one-half of black men (60.3%) and women (51.2%) from 25 to 29 years of age have never married compared to about two-fifths of white (43.6%) and Hispanic (44.5%) males and about one-fourth of white (25.9%) and Hispanic (24.8%) females.[22]

This represents a remarkable social change among the younger cohorts of Americans, since there is some evidence that a small proportion of adults—blacks more than whites—are choosing singlehood as an enduring life-style. Still, most (93.1%) white women and a large proportion (78.5%) of black women do marry at least once in their lifetime. Delays in marriage permit women to develop a strong work orientation, one that persists after marriage and motherhood. These trends suggest that today young American women are no longer looking to marriage for financial security, but expect to earn their own living.

Trends in Female-Headed Families

In 1988, one in five families with children present in the United States was maintained by a single-parent mother (Bureau of Labor Statistics 1989). The proportion of such families doubled between 1970 and 1988 (from 9.9% to 19.7%) as a result of rising divorce rates and of the increasing numbers of children born out of wedlock. The divorce rate in 1988 was 4.8 per 1,000 population, markedly higher than the low of 2.1 in 1958 and down only slightly from the high watermark of 5.3 reached in 1979 and again in 1981. In 1970 about one in ten (10.7%) children was born to an unmarried woman; by 1987 about one of every four (24.5%) children was born out of wedlock. Three out of every five black births were to unmarried women, compared to less than one in five white births.[23]

These changes in divorce and nonmarital fertility have led to an ever larger number of families with children maintained by single-parent mothers, reaching one in five of all American families by 1988. The trends are especially striking in the case of black families; in 1987, almost one in two (48.4%) black families was headed by a woman (see Figure 2.8).

Trends in Wages and Poverty

Traditionally in the United States a man's wage has been regarded as a family wage, sufficient to support his wife and children, as well as himself. However, there has been a steady decline in real earnings (controlling for inflation), especially for low wage earners, so that a single salary today is insufficient to maintain a satisfactory standard of living for most families in the United States. Add to this the fact that most Americans aspire to an ever higher quality of life, and the employment of wives and mothers becomes essential. For example, in 1970 almost half (47%) of working women interviewed said they were working "to bring in extra money." By 1990 only 27 percent gave this

Figure 2.8
Trends in Families with Children under 18 Present Maintained by Women, by Race, 1960–1987

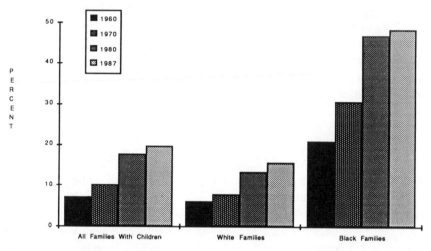

Sources: U.S. Bureau of the Census 1989: 38.

reason. In 1990 fully 55 percent said they were working to support themselves and their families, up from 46 percent just ten years earlier.[24]

Jobs are even more critical to women who are rearing children on their own. In 1987, 45 percent of families with children headed by women were living in poverty, compared to only 7 percent of married couple families. Contributing to the problem is the fact that most single-parent women receive little or no financial support from the fathers of their children. In 1985, 25 percent of working, single-parent mothers received no child support payments owed by the child's father, and 40 percent were not awarded any child support payment whatsoever (O'Connell and Bloom 1987:2).[25]

The cultural contradictions and ambivalence surrounding working mothers are most dramatic and most devastating in the case of single-parent mothers. Women earn significantly less than men in part because historically they have not been the family breadwinners. Public attitudes regarding women's roles, as well as discrimination, have channeled many women into low-wage, insecure, often temporary or dead-end, jobs. This low-earning status fits with traditional notions of women as the caretakers of children who, if employed, work only for "pin" money. But the notion is at odds with contemporary egalitarian views and the reality of women as family breadwinners. The curious coupling of these old and new views of gender roles characterizes a society in which single-parent women are disproportionately responsible for the custody and support of their children, but where alimony is old-fashioned and child support awards are both inadequate and unenforced and where single mothers often have great difficulty making ends meet even when employed full-time. These conditions, in turn, necessarily inflate welfare rolls; unprecedented numbers of children are now supported by Aid to Families with Dependent Children (AFDC).

What solutions to this problem were proposed by government in the 1980s and early 1990s? The principal strategy advocated on both sides of the legislative aisle was to get "welfare mothers" employed. But to do so without also remedying the problems of low wage rates, occupational segregation, and unmet child-care needs only exacerbates the dilemmas of single-parent women.

The Changing Shape of Childhood

Transformations in the roles of women have meant corresponding changes in the demography of childhood. Children today are likely to have fewer brothers and sisters, as well as more educated mothers, than did those of previous generations. They also are more apt to have working mothers (see Figure 2.9).

The changing life-styles of adults have led to declining numbers of children living with both parents, and growing numbers—one in five—live in single-parent families. Here there have been marked differences by race (see Figure 2.10). In 1987 only 40 percent of black children lived with two parents, compared to 80 percent of white children and 66 percent of Hispanic children. These proportions have shifted downward even in the short period since 1970 when 90 percent of white and 59 percent of black children lived with two parents. Most strikingly, an estimated seven out of ten white children and nine out of every ten black children born in 1980 will spend some portion of their childhood in a single-parent family (U.S. Bureau of the Census 1990a).[26]

OUTLOOK FOR THE FUTURE

Many women find it extremely difficult to decide whether they are mothers who happen to work, or workers who happen to be mothers. (O'Connell and Bloom 1987:5)

Figure 2.9
Trends in Preschoolers (0 to 5) with Parent at Home or Working Parents, 1940–1988

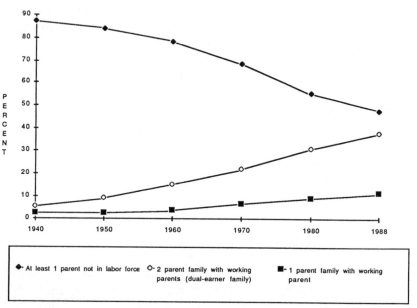

Legend:
◆· At least 1 parent not in labor force   O· 2 parent family with working parents (dual-earner family)   ■· 1 parent family with working parent

Source: Adapted from Hernandez 1992.

The social and demographic transformations discussed in this chapter are not separate, isolated events. Reductions and delays in fertility and marriage, increases in single parenthood and educational achievement—along with the women's movement, declining real wages, and the specter of poverty—all encourage, facilitate, or even necessitate the employment of women, including mothers of young children.

But women remain at a disadvantage in the workplace. The downside of maternal employment involves more than the experience of role overloads, strains, and conflicts. For many women it also includes low earnings, few employment benefits, and little job security. These conditions frequently characterize the kinds of jobs that provide the flexibility mothers must have to manage work and family obligations. Feminist scholars attribute much of the economic disadvantage of American women and their children to the perpetuation of traditional gender-role distinctions that result in policies and practices designed for the traditional male breadwinner. These roles render women central to home and family but peripheral to employment.[27] While the employment of wives

Figure 2.10
Trends in Children under 18 Living with Mother Only, by Race,
1970–1987

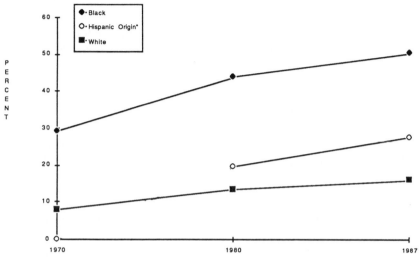

Source: U.S. Bureau of the Census 1989: 52.
*Persons of Hispanic origin may be of any race.

is increasingly accepted, many Americans remain ambivalent about the employment of mothers of young children.

Nevertheless, employment has become, and doubtlessly will continue to be, a fact of contemporary life for most wives and mothers, their husbands, and their children. The tide of time and events surrounding this most striking social change challenges traditional notions of motherhood, childhood, and gender. But we as a society have yet to come to terms with the inconsistencies and contradictions that grow out of the uneven changes in our culture, in our institutions, and, indeed, in the lives of contemporary American men and women.

NOTES

1. While relatively few women were involved in the labor force at any one point in time, employment was commonplace in the early years of women's lives prior to World War II. Over 90 percent of urban women born in 1915 are estimated to have entered the labor force by 1938; however, following the custom of the times, most left their jobs after marriage or the birth of their first child (Campbell 1984).

2. See Chafe (1972) and Campbell (1984). For a life cycle approach that suggests that the preconditions for the expansion following the war were set well before the war, see Goldin (1983).

3. See the discussion by Hochschild (1983) about the emotional work of women. A number of writers have analyzed the experiences of women during and after World War II (Anderson 1981; Banner 1974; Campbell 1984; Chafe 1972; Evans 1989; Kaledin 1984; Margolis 1984; Oppenheimer 1970; Women's Bureau 1946). For a broader historical view, see Scott and Tilly (1975). For statistical data on changes in women's employment, see Shank (1988).

4. Personal communication, Howard Hayghe (1991) from the Bureau of Labor Statistics on data for the second quarter of 1990; see also Bureau of Labor Statistics (1989). At the same time that women's involvement in paid employment began to climb, men's labor force participation began to decline; their rate dropped from 86.8 percent in 1947 to 76.7 percent in 1985 as men increasingly opted for earlier retirement (U.S. Bureau of the Census 1975b, 1986).

5. This drop in the median age is even more striking, given the aging of the population.

6. See U.S. Bureau of the Census (1975b), Bureau of Labor Statistics (1989), and Farley (1984).

7. See U.S. Bureau of the Census (1990b).

8. This draws on data contained in O'Connell and Bloom (1987).

9. See Ryan (1975). The 1938 opinion polls are discussed by Banner (1974) and by Spitze and Huber (1980).

10. See research reported in Mason, Czajka, and Arber (1976), Duncan and Duncan (1978), and Spitze and Huber (1980).

11. Surprisingly, all except the youngest cohorts of women experienced a decline in the proportions approving the employment of wives from 1972 to 1977. See Spitze and Huber (1980) and Mason and Lu (1988).

12. Survey data show that older, black women (who were born before 1930) tended to be more liberal than white women of the same age. Younger women with more education are also less traditional than older women or those with less education. Survey findings from the 1970s suggest that a shift to egalitarianism occurred among whites, but few changes took place among blacks, who were already less traditional in their attitudes. There also was a major shift in *men's* sex-role attitudes; by 1978, there was little difference in the proportions of men and women who approved of married women working (Cherlin and Walters 1981).

13. The 1985 data come from the Virginia Slims Opinion Poll. The 1989 data come from a *New York Times* poll (unpublished data).

14. Findings that employment affected attitudes were reported in Molm (1978); findings showing that attitudes affected employment are reported in Macke and Morgan (1978) and Spitze and Waite (1981b).

15. See Miller and Garrison (1982:246).

16. For information about the Women's Movement, see Wandersee (1988) and Chafetz and Dworkin (1986). For an overview of the changes in women's lives, see McLaughlin et al. (1988) and Bianchi and Spain (1986).

17. Data are derived from the Statistical Abstract of the United States (U.S. Bureau of the Census 1990b:65).

18. For women aged 30 to 34, the births per 1,000 women were 56.4 in 1976 and 81.9 in 1988. For women aged 35 to 39, the births per 1,000 women were 22.6 in 1976 and 33.6 in 1988 (U.S. Bureau of the Census 1990b).

19. See U.S. Bureau of the Census (1990b:69) and Bureau of Labor Statistics (1988). The direction of causality between fertility and employment has captured the interest of demographers, whose consensus is that women's employment plans negatively constrain their fertility plans. But the cause-and-effect answer is not that simple. Most likely, women make a succession of interrelated if not simultaneous decisions regarding the nature, timing, and duration of their family and work roles. Hence, family plans are apt to affect employment decisions, just as employment plans seem to affect fertility decisions (Morgan and Waite 1987; Stolzenberg and Waite 1977; Waite, Haggstrom, and Kanouse 1985; Felmlee 1984).

20. In 1970 the participation rate for those with less than a high school education was 43.0; by 1988 it was 45.4. In 1988 the proportions were 45.4 and 80.8 (U.S. Bureau of the Census 1990b).

21. The 1950s median age at first marriage was the lowest recorded in this century (U.S. Bureau of the Census 1990a; Espenshade 1985; Cherlin 1980; Modell 1986).

22. These data come from the U.S. Bureau of the Census (1990a). There has also been an increase in the number of unmarried-couple households, from 523,000 in 1970 to 2.8 million in 1989.

23. See U.S. Bureau of the Census (1990b). The percent of all births to unmarried black women in 1987 was 62.2; to white women, 16.7.

24. Data come from *New York Times* polls and the Virginia Slims Opinion Poll (Belkin 1989; Cowan 1989; Townsend and O'Neil 1990). In 1983, 35 percent of working women in a nationwide survey said that, if they lost their jobs tomorrow, it would have a major financial impact on themselves and on their families; by 1989, 45 percent of the women interviewed (compared to 44 percent of the men interviewed about losing their jobs) gave this reason. Oppenheimer (1982) provides a discussion of the importance of women's earnings to the family economy.

25. For additional information, see Cherlin (1981), Garfinkel and McLanahan (1986), Farley (1984).

26. By 1986 only 40 percent of preschoolers had mothers who were married, full-time homemakers. Even fewer (28.7%) school-aged children fit this traditional family situation (Hofferth 1985; Espenshade 1985).

27. See, for example, England and Farkas (1986), Garfinkel and McLanahan (1986), Hartmann (1981), Huber and Spitze (1983), Reskin (1988), Sokoloff (1980, 1988).

II Consequences

3 PATTERNS, PROBLEMS, AND PAYOFFS FOR WOMEN

All women, for whom that marriage-and-childbearing "destiny" used to be the main source of identity, prestige, financial support, have suffered an apocalyptic change in their being. They can't escape that change.

(Friedan 1981:316)

As early as the 1940s sociologist Mirra Komarovsky (1946, 1953) recounted the "cultural contradictions" of educated women. Society, through husbands, friends, and kin, sent mixed messages: Be career oriented but also be a paragon of domesticity. Women today—at all educational levels—still confront these conflicting expectations (Gerson 1985, 1987; Hochschild 1989). The quandary they face is not employment, but *combining* employment with motherhood. Since women continue to be the principal caretakers of children, how do they mesh work and family roles over the course of their lives? Are contemporary women—juggling these two, as well as other, roles—better or worse off than the traditional full-time housewives of the 1950s?

MANAGING WORK AND FAMILY ROLES OVER THE LIFE COURSE

The decade between age 25 and 35 is when all lawyers become partners in the good firms, when business managers make it onto the "fast track," when academics get tenure at good universities, and when blue collar workers find the training opportunities and the skills that will generate high earnings. But [this] . . . is precisely the decade when women are most apt to leave the labor force or become part-time workers to have children. When they do, the current system of promotion and skill acquisition will extract an enormous lifetime price. (Thurow 1984:42)

The figures included in Chapter 2 paint in broad strokes the upward trends in women's employment at all stages of their lives. What these statistics fail to portray are the experiences of *individuals* as they become mothers and raise their children. To understand what these long-term trends mean for individual women requires a "life course" perspective.[1] This approach underscores the continuous interplay between work and family roles throughout women's lives, as well as the historical changes in working and parenting. From the 1940s through the 1980s, the picture that emerges is one of continuity in women's accommodation of work to family roles, despite increases in the portion of their adulthood they spend in employment. The timing and duration of women's work roles may have changed, but their family roles continue to take precedence over work. What *has* changed is the nature of these accommodations.

Accommodating Work to Family

Recall that, following World War II, women typically resolved potential conflicts between work and family obligations by scheduling them *sequentially*, leaving their jobs when they married or with the birth of their first child and returning to work when their children grew older. In fact, from the 1940s through the 1960s the best predictors of whether or not a woman was employed were the number and ages of her children.[2] Child-care responsibilities still constrain *uninterrupted* employment, and significant numbers of women continue to withdraw from the labor force when their children are small.[3] One prominent example is Associate Supreme Court Justice Sandra Day O'Connor, who took five years "off" from the practice of law following the birth of her second child. She recalls that, at the time, she was "worried that it would be hard to get back into the practice of law" (Chion-Kinney 1988:C5). This sequential pattern obviously did not hinder Justice O'Connor's career, but for many other women it can be extremely damaging. Women's growing recognition of the disruptive effects of leaving and later reentering employment—in pay, job security, and career advancement—has resulted in a steady decline, since the 1950s, in the amount of time they spend out of the labor force while their children are young.

A second strategy for resolving work/family cross-pressures has been to remain employed while raising preschoolers but to cut back on the hours worked.[4] In most jobs in the United States, however, work time cannot be reduced, temporarily or permanently, to fewer than thirty-five hours a week (the standard definition of full time). Consequently, many women wanting to work fewer hours have had to abandon their full-time jobs for more marginal part-time work and take jobs that typically provide less pay and few if any benefits (including health insurance and pensions), no seniority protection or employment security, and little opportunity for upward mobility.[5]

Part-time work is typically a short-term expedient for most women. In my study of a national sample of women in the 1970s, I found few who worked part-time for as many as five consecutive years, but over half of those who worked at all were employed part-time at least one year out of five. The women most likely to move in and out of part-time employment and in and out of the labor force were those with some college education who also were mothers of preschoolers (Moen 1985). Part-time employment, particularly on an intermittent basis, continues today as an important means for mothers of young children to maintain some degree of attachment to the labor force. On the other hand, it reinforces their continued economic dependence, on their husband's earnings or on government welfare payments, and it is not a viable option for many working-class women who cannot afford to work fewer hours and reduce their family income.[6]

A third strategy for managing the competing pressures of work and family is shift work. Employed mothers, especially those who are married, frequently opt for nonstandard working hours so that both parents can jointly coordinate child care. In fact, in 1985, in about one-third of the dual-earner families with preschoolers—where both parents held full-time jobs—either the mother or the father worked an evening, night, or rotating shift. However, it is the mothers more than the fathers who adapt their work schedules for care giving; they are five times more likely to cite child care as the reason for working evenings or nights.[7]

A fourth, and more subtle, strategy for accommodating work and family roles is through the selection of less involving occupations. In 1953, Mirra Komarovsky prescribed an "undemanding" job as the solution to the pressures faced by working mothers. Such a tack is taken by many women today who choose to reject or abandon the "fast track" of occupational achievement and career progression in order to tend to family needs. One mother who chose this accommodation strategy reports: "I gave up traveling when I had my first child. The other alternative would have been to have a live-in babysitter. . . . I found a job that didn't demand that I travel. So I try very hard to have breakfast with them in the morning, then go to work, and come home—leave the office promptly at five" (Hertz 1986:141). Survey data suggest that this strategy is widely used, with fathers more likely than mothers to travel on the job and mothers more likely than fathers to take time off for family emergencies. For example, almost half of the fathers interviewed in 1986 reported traveling out of town as part of their job, regardless of whether their wives were employed. By contrast, only 23 percent of the employed married mothers and 15 percent of the single-parent mothers traveled on the job. Over one-fifth of the fathers were away from home overnight one or more nights a month, compared to less than one in ten employed mothers. Moreover, 71 percent of the mothers in two-earner families reported taking time off from work to handle a family emergency, such as the sudden illness of a child, in contrast to only 15 percent of the fathers in these families (Opinion Research Corporation 1987).

These findings lend credence to social psychologist Joseph Pleck's observation: Men's work spills over into their family life; women's family obligations spill over into their work (Pleck 1977).

Reducing working hours, moving to a less demanding job or to shift work, and leaving the job entirely are all ways women use to manage conflicting work and family responsibilities. These options, however, are seldom open to single-parent mothers. Given the uncertainty and insufficiency of child support payments, mothers raising children on their own must either work full-time or fall back on welfare support. Black single-parent mothers traditionally have relied on relatives to help with child care so that they could work full-time. However, increasingly, their mothers, sisters, and other family members have jobs themselves and are now less available for babysitting and child care.[8]

Accommodating Family to Work

Thus far I have discussed only one side of the work/family equation— ways used by working mothers to reduce or arrange the time demands of their *jobs*. There is a reciprocal strategy, increasingly common, that involves reducing the demands of *family life*. By delaying childbearing or having fewer children, women can make a greater investment in employment (cf. Davis and Van den Oever 1982; Davis 1984). This "solution" was already apparent in the baby boom era of the 1950s:

The working mother and the mother of four or more children were two responses to the same social changes. . . . They were, however, alternative responses;

that is, both rates were rising but the employed mothers had fewer children. (Hoffman 1975:106-7)

As the statistics presented in Chapter 2 suggest, having fewer children and delaying motherhood are increasingly popular strategies for reconciling the competing agendas of work and family. However, unless women reject motherhood entirely, having fewer children and having them later in life only reduces, not eliminates, the work/family conflict.[9]

Still another widespread means of reducing family pressures is through the purchase of products and services that women previously provided at home. More Americans are now eating out more than ever before, and frozen dinners quickly prepared in the microwave oven are becoming a staple in many households. These and other tactics—such as having laundry done out of the home—permit working families to buy themselves more "free" time.

Short-Term Remedies, Long-Term Costs

From the 1970s on there has been no standard pattern of meshing work and family that characterizes women's lives. Before that time the accepted practice was, if at all possible, to sequence paid work prior to and after family obligations. Today's wives and mothers continue to accommodate work to family, but they now adopt a range of strategies: sandwiching paid work around family responsibilities by leaving their jobs for (progressively smaller) periods of time, moving to part-time employment or shift work, or choosing a more flexible, less demanding job. Women have made—and doubtlessly will continue to make—occupational decisions that permit them to blend both work and family roles rather than pursue exclusively career goals. This was true of women who obtained professional degrees in the mid-1940s, and it now is the practice of a large proportion of women in all walks of life.[10]

Given the absence of institutional arrangements to ease the strains of working parents (such as child care, parental leaves, and flexible time on the job), as well as prevailing social attitudes about child care as "women's work," mothers in the 1990s, like those in earlier decades, combine a variety of ad hoc personal strategies to manage their work and family obligations.

Giving priority to family roles impedes most women's long-term occupational progress. What one husband of a corporate professional says is suggestive of what many believe:

We both wanted a family—two kids—and when the kids entered the picture it obviously became more difficult to keep all these things in the air—two kids and two careers. Our decision was to run to the more traditional, where my wife would have the major responsibility for the direction of the kids until they were in school. As a result she is limping along in terms of her career. We talked about it. But I have personally never seriously considered severing my career, at any stage, to stay home with the kids like Janet would. (Hertz 1986:137)

The way that women have typically put work on the back burner while their children are young has been costly in terms of their upward mobility, earning power, job security, and occupational achievement. This was the reality in the 1950s and it continues to hold true today (cf. Yohalem 1979; Rosenfeld 1978, 1980). An in-depth study conducted in the 1970s of a small sample of new mothers found that most continued to take time out of the labor force when their first child was born (Daniels and Weingarten 1982). Those who tried to manage motherhood and employment simultaneously were typically the "late-timers," women who delayed childbearing until they became launched in their careers. For all the women in the study, however, the transition to parenthood inevitably affected their work lives, but not the work lives of their husbands.

There also is a more subjective side to employment: the commitment to work women feel and its impact on women's psychological well-being.

COMMITMENT TO WORK

Working mothers—whether in the 1950s or the 1990s—are a very diverse group. Consider these four broad categories: captives, conflicted, copers, and committed.

Captives

Captives are people who unwillingly or reluctantly perform particular roles. According to Pearlin (1983), the hallmark of role captivity consists of the unwilling engagement in particular roles. Working mothers who would prefer to be full-time homemakers illustrate one form of this captivity. These may be single parents who are sole breadwinners, wives of blue-collar workers whose own incomes are crucial to the family economy, or part of the increasing group of middle-class women who find two salaries necessary to achieve a desired standard of living (Rainwater 1974). Regardless of how well these women like their jobs, they find their family responsibilities—in conjunction with paid work—overwhelming and remain in the labor force reluctantly.

Until recently the public generally regarded most working mothers of preschoolers as captives. In fact, statements are still commonly heard about women working "because they have to," implying that in the absence of financial need most working mothers would stay home.

In all likelihood the proportion of captives among working mothers has declined over the last four decades. Whitham and Moen (1992) found, in the 1950s in upstate New York, that 47 percent of the working mothers interviewed in 1956 preferred to be full-time homemakers, and only 12 percent of the homemakers preferred to be employed. By contrast, twenty years later, in another community study—this time in Detroit—just over 40 percent of the housewives would have liked to have had jobs.[11]

Conflicted

Numerous employed mothers express ambivalence about their two roles as mother and as worker. These are women who, although they are in the labor force themselves, feel that the employment of mothers is "harmful to children." They are subject to substantial cross-pressures, trying to be both good mothers and good workers. If all goes well—the car starts, a child is not sick, the clothes washer does not break, child-care arrangements are reliable—they may just succeed.

But when things go wrong, they may find it exceedingly difficult to manage both roles successfully. These are the women who are likely to leave the labor force while their children are young. Many voluntarily quit work if they can afford it. However, one study found that the presence of preschoolers increased the rate at which women are fired or laid off from their jobs, suggesting that employers sometimes take the initiative when women's family responsibilities detract from their work performance.[12]

In the 1950s and 1960s these women probably would have delayed going back to work until their children were older. But by the 1970s, 1980s, and 1990s, women were increasingly combining work and family roles, for both economic and personal reasons, despite the juggling act required.

Copers

Women who successfully manage to work while their children are young typically do so either by reducing the demands of one (or both) of their roles or by prioritizing them. These are, most commonly, women with only one or two children who choose jobs with enough flexibility to accommodate to family concerns. Some manage by reducing their daily or weekly working hours or by leaving the labor force for brief periods. Their aim, in effect, is to reduce the "costs" of employment to their families. In the 1990s, as in the 1950s, this often means settling for minimally demanding jobs. But, as previously noted, women pay a price for these short-term solutions—first by accepting lower wages and fewer benefits and, in the long run, by forgoing promotional opportunities, seniority advantages, and pay progression.

Committed

An informal 1991 survey of female college students conducted at Cornell University revealed that many held high occupational aspirations coupled with a strong commitment to marriage and family life. These contemporary young women declared their ambition to be successful doctors, lawyers, and executives by the time they are in their 30s *and* to marry and to have as many as three children! Because of their (and their parents') substantial investment in education they are unwilling to sacrifice career for family. But it would appear that they are equally unwilling to sacrifice family for career. Their model is the mother who has but one or two children, relatively late in life, and who can afford to pay for whatever child care is required, including normally expensive live-in arrangements, in order to pursue her own career goals.[13]

Most social scientists who study working mothers center their attention on these "committed" women. This is understandable since these researchers themselves often have dual-career marriages and are absorbed by their own life-style. But professional women constitute only a minuscule proportion of the female work force (Moen and Dempster-McClain 1987). Most women fall into the categories of copers and conflicted—with a dual allegiance to work and family and a patchwork arrangement for accommodating one to the other.

Trends

The available evidence suggests that fewer working mothers are role captives today than ever before and, correspondingly, that there are growing numbers of committed, work-oriented women at all occupational levels. A nationwide poll conducted in 1989 by the *New York Times* suggests that cohort differences exist in work orientation. For example,

55 percent of women 18–44 would prefer to combine marriage, children, and a career, while only 50 percent of those over 45 would like to combine work and family roles. Most of the younger women (56%) but less than half of those over 45 (40%) believed that men's attitudes toward women have changed for the better in the past twenty years. Still, over half of both age groups (57% of those 18–44 and 54% of those over 45) agreed that men are willing to let women get ahead, but only if women still do all the housework at home (Belkin 1989). A 1990 national poll found that 45 percent of women think of their work as a career, up from 41 percent in 1985 (Townsend and O'Neil 1990). One conclusion is inescapable: Increasing numbers of women intend to combine employment and family roles throughout adulthood.

Evidence of a decline in women's preference for full-time homemaking is provided by surveys conducted twenty years apart, in 1957 and 1976. Over 20 percent of the working wives in 1957 said they would prefer to be homemakers exclusively; by 1976 only 3 percent of a similar sample expressed such a preference. Similarly, only 17 percent of the homemakers in 1957 wished to work outside the home sometime in the future, compared to 37 percent in 1976 (Townsend and Gurin 1981). Major changes occurred in the early 1970s. In 1969, for example, only 56 percent of a sample of college women aimed to blend both roles; only four years later, 63 percent of a similar sample expected to do so (Parelius 1975). Even more striking is the change in the proportions of women who planned on continuous, uninterrupted labor force participation: in 1969, 16 percent and in 1973, 37 percent. In 1990, 57 percent of women reported that combining marriage, career, and children was the ideal life-style; only 27 percent preferred marriage and children, but no career (Townsend and O'Neil 1990).

Signs of the approaching obsolescence of continuous full-time homemaking as a permanent life-style can be found in trends in college freshmen's attitudes toward women's roles. Recall from Chapter 2 (Figure 2.4) that 44 percent of women entering college in 1967 endorsed the view that "the activities of married women are best confined to the home and family." But by 1988 this support for women's traditional role was expressed by only 20 percent. The career and work plans of these younger women, in conjunction with their more egalitarian attitudes, suggest that a major social change has occurred as a result of cohort replacement, that is, younger women supplanting older ones. Working women who are captives, who would prefer *not* to be employed, may soon be uncommon—prevalent in the 1950s but novel in the 1990s. Still, large numbers of women (and a minority of men), although committed to employment, may want to take time off to raise their children or to reduce their working hours during the child-rearing years. In another *New York Times* poll conducted in 1989 almost half (49%) of the women and a third (33%) of the men interviewed felt that women have had to give up too much to get better jobs and more opportunities than they had twenty years ago (Cowan 1989). Whether future generations of working mothers will be conflicted, copers, or committed depends to a large extent on the supports provided—by husbands, employers, and government—to enable them to succeed both at work and at home.

EMPLOYMENT AND WELL-BEING

In order to understand the relevance of either homemaking or outside employment to depression, we must look at the meanings of these roles for people and at the conditions that are encountered within the roles. (Pearlin 1975:196)

Consider these important findings, each consistent across different time periods. First, on almost every measure of psychological well-being, men, especially married men, score higher than women, especially married women. Studies from the 1950s through the 1980s uniformly document this gender difference.[14] Second, men are more likely to be employed than are women.[15] Third, having young children in the home adversely affects the emotional well-being of parents, particularly mothers, and single parents are especially vulnerable.[16] What then is the relationship between the employment of mothers of young children and their psychological well-being?

Social scientists have long recognized the significance of employment in the lives of men as the most fundamental source of personal identity and fulfillment. As D. J. Levinson points out, "[A] man's work is the primary base for his life in society. [Through it he is] plugged into an occupational structure and a cultural, class and social matrix. Work is also of great psychological importance; it is a vehicle for the fulfillment or negation of central aspects of the self" (1978:8). Until recently, research on women focused almost exclusively on marriage and mothering as central to their identity and to their mental health. When researchers did consider women's employment, they tended to focus on the possible liabilities of combining work and family roles. That men typically combine work and family—most work and most also become fathers—was taken as a given and seen not as problematic but possibly even beneficial to them (Long and Porter 1984).

In fact, some sociologists argue that men gain advantage from their work roles—in the form of status, social relationships, and self-esteem. Women, by contrast, have been more vulnerable to psychological distress; until recently, they have been hemmed in by their exclusive homemaking responsibilities.[17] However, as women become more "like men" (i.e., employed for most of their adult lives), the argument goes, they too will benefit psychologically. Thus, from this *role accumulation* perspective, employed mothers and wives should experience higher levels of well-being than women who are exclusively homemakers.[18]

On the other hand, there are those who favor a *role strain* interpretation and make an opposite argument.[19] According to this view, maternal employment is detrimental to women's psychological well-being because it introduces competing demands on time, energy, and involvement. Proponents of the role strain position argue that combining work and family roles is more stressful for women than it is for men because women take on employment *over and above* their domestic obligations, whereas men remain free to concentrate almost exclusively on their work.[20] This perspective particularly pinpoints the difficulties women experience in the early years of child rearing, since young working mothers must deal simultaneously with the extraordinary demands of preschoolers and the day-to-day requirements of their jobs. Mothers who are captives or conflicted best illustrate this role strain viewpoint.

The relative validity of the role strain and the role accumulation interpretations is difficult to gauge inasmuch as research has produced conflicting findings. Moreover, most studies examining the effects of employment on women ignore possibly important differences among them in age, socioeconomic level, marital status, and family stage. The findings of research on women in general may well obscure the still more specific effects of employment on mothers, particularly mothers of young children. Nevertheless, I will describe the more general case because it represents the current state of knowledge in the field. I will then follow with a summary of what researchers have learned about mothers of young children, the group most vulnerable to the most intense cross-pressures.

Psychological Well-Being

Indexes of personal well-being commonly incorporate various symptoms of psychological distress. Assessing trends in well-being or quality of life as a global state is complicated because it involves both objective (life-style) and subjective (psychological) components (Baruch 1984; Campbell, Converse, and Rodgers 1976; Warr and Parry 1982). Maternal employment, by adding to the household income, does permit families to improve, or at least to maintain, their material standard of living. But whether the upturn in maternal employment has contributed to an improvement in women's *feelings* of well-being is far less obvious.

Social researchers use numerous measures of psychological well-being, such as happiness and satisfaction, positive and negative feelings, psychological distress, daily fatigue, depressive symptoms, anxiety, psychiatric impairment, unhappiness, strain, personal inadequacy, mood, mastery, and pleasure. Consequently, variations found in the relationship between women's employment and their psychological well-being or in shifts in well-being over time may well reflect differences in the measures chosen.

Research findings most often relate employment to lower levels of distress, although a few studies find more distress among working women, and still others reveal no differences in the psychological well-being of women who are full-time homemakers and those who are in the labor force.[21] Other studies measure women's overall life satisfaction, but they offer no clear evidence, in either direction, about the effects of employment on satisfaction.

For example, Angus Campbell (1982), in examining nationwide data collected in 1978, found no difference whatsoever in psychological well-being in relation to educational level. A comparison made of wives in 1957 and 1976 discloses little difference in either period between the proportions of employed and nonemployed women who report life satisfaction (Iglehart 1979). Another large-scale survey conducted in 1973 found no statistically significant association between happiness and employment status (Spreitzer, Snyder, and Larson 1975). Still another 1976 replication of a 1957 survey (Americans View Their Mental Health) did report that homemakers were slightly happier than women in the labor force, but that the effects of neither homemaking nor employment had changed from 1957 to 1976 (Veroff, Douvan, and Kulka 1981). One nationwide survey undertaken in 1971 found no difference in either happiness or satisfaction between employed and nonemployed women, except in the case of college-educated women, who were more likely to report general life satisfaction and happiness if they were in the labor force (Campbell, Converse, and Rodgers 1976). A smaller study of Boston area women found no difference by labor force status in the happiness, satisfaction, and optimism of women aged from 35 to 55 but reported, at the same time, that employed women had both a higher self-concept and fewer symptoms of psychological distress than those out of the labor force. Full-time housewives were more likely to be dissatisfied with their lives, even though the working mothers were principally involved in lower level clerical, factory, sales, and service jobs (Baruch 1984; Baruch, Barnett, and Rivers 1984). In an attempt to tease out the relationship between employment and life satisfaction, James Wright examined data from six national surveys conducted between 1971 and 1976, focusing on a subsample of white married women. He concludes that "both work outside the home and full-time housewifery have benefits and costs attached to them; the net result is that there is no consistent or significant differences in patterns of life satisfaction between the two groups" (1978: 301). Unfortunately, however, working women with preschool children, a critically important group, were omitted from Wright's analyses.

Some scholars suggest that one cannot determine the psychological effects of employment without taking into account women's *attitudes*. Whether women are captives to employment, conflicted about their work and family obligations, coping with these two roles, or committed exclusively to their careers makes an enormous difference on the impact of paid work on their well-being. Studies have shown that the women who accept employment and enjoy their jobs (the copers and the committed) are the most likely to benefit from employment.[22] In upstate New York, even at the height of the family-oriented 1950s, the captives—employed mothers who would prefer to be at home and full-time homemakers who would prefer to be at work—were *both* less likely to be satisfied with their lives than women who were following the life-style they preferred (Whitham and Moen 1992). Similarly, a 1972 study found that career-oriented homemakers, that is, those with career goals, were the most likely to express dissatisfaction with their lives (Townsend and Gurin 1981). Still more recent data confirm that congruency between personal orientations and employment status is an important determinant of women's well-being, as are their husbands' attitudes toward women's roles.[23]

But the issue is more complicated yet. Women whose husbands assist with domestic responsibilities (housework, child care) are the most likely to benefit psychologically from employment. Child-care help seems to be the most critical factor, as evident in a 1976 nationwide survey finding that employment enhanced the psychological well-being only of women whose husbands shared in child care.[24]

Still another vital consideration is the nature of the jobs that women hold. Whether employment positively or negatively affects well-being depends on the characteristics of the job and the conditions of work. While mothers of young children have increasingly entered the labor force, relatively few have come to hold "men's" jobs. Their paid work, of course, is *in addition* to the domestic work they perform in fulfilling their traditional and principal role of care giving, of children particularly, but also of the home and the family more generally. Consequently, the effects of employment may well be different for women than for men, and the conditions of employment that are obstacles to fulfilling family responsibilities can be expected to have detrimental effects on the well-being of employed mothers.

Investigators report that prestige (Kessler and Cleary 1980), the absence of physical and psychological pressures (Moen 1989; Miller et al. 1979), work history (Belle 1982), and degree of challenge or self-direction (Miller et al. 1979; Baruch, Barnett, and Rivers 1984) all enhance well-being—for women as well as men. The level of income does not appreciably affect women, except that high-income women with little help from their husbands in child care and housework tend to experience more anxiety than those with lower earnings (Cleary and Mechanic 1983; Kessler and McRae 1982). Unlike with men, part-time employment is associated with higher levels of well-being among women, since it presumably permits a better coordination of work and family responsibilities (Lennon 1987; Moen 1989; Moen and Forest 1990; Spreitzer, Snyder, and Larson 1975). Sarah Rosenfield (1989) points to the need to consider both family and work demands in assessing the effects of employment on well-being. Other studies also point to the importance of the quality of the role experience (Kandel, Davies, and Raveis 1985; Baruch and Barnett 1987).

Few studies of the psychological consequences of employment have examined racial or ethnic differences,[25] and studies of the influence of social class have yielded ambiguous results. Warr and Parry (1982) found that employment was more beneficial to middle-class women than to working-class women (see also Baruch, Barnett, and Rivers 1984). However, other studies report dissimilar results. Pearlin (1975), for example, notes that career-oriented middle-class women with high family obligations are more prone to role conflict and, hence, depression than are working-class women. In a study of urban Canadian women, Welch and Booth (1977) found that women in working-class families who were employed full time for at least one year reported the fewest symptoms of depression and anxiety. Ferree (1976) and Belle (1982) also report that employment has salutary effects on working-class women. But, as testimony to the complexity of the picture, Kessler and McRae (1982) found that women earning high incomes who also had child-care responsibilities were less likely to be depressed but more apt to be anxious than were those at lower socioeconomic levels.

Employment for women without children or for those whose children are grown may have quite different consequences than does employment for mothers of young children. A national study conducted in the 1960s of young college-educated women found that those who were involved exclusively in family and child rearing had higher levels of self-esteem than did women following a less typical career-oriented life-style. However, sociologist Alice Rossi (1965) suggested that the relative levels of self-esteem would be reversed as these women moved into middle and later adulthood. A study conducted by Judith Birnbaum (1975) of a small number (N = 81) of upper middle-class women who had graduated from college fifteen to twenty-five years earlier provides corroborating evidence. Birnbaum found that, in mid-life, employed professional women, whether married or single, had higher levels of self-esteem than did full-time homemakers.

Unfortunately, most studies linking employment to well-being do not consider the stage of the life course but, rather, treat women from 18 to 65 as a homogeneous group. Those few studies that do take into account the presence and age of children find that employed mothers of young children are particularly vulnerable to role overload and strains, given their heavy family obligations.[26] However, other studies have not confirmed the greater likelihood of strains among employed mothers of young children.[27] Recall that, when a husband helps with child care, employment is more likely to have a positive effect on a woman's well-being (Kessler and McRae 1982).

Since the United States is in a process of transition it seems logical that the effects of employment on women's well-being may also be in transition. As the employment of mothers of young children becomes commonplace and as more and more women choose to work, the benefits may well outweigh the inevitable costs of combining two jobs. The evidence suggests that a strong commitment to employment, structural flexibilities and challenges on the job, and support at home all encourage positive outcomes.

Isolation

Most research to date has examined the influence of employment on well-being; few investigators look at the obverse: how full-time *homemaking* affects women's psychological health. The general consensus of those studying the role of the housewife is that it offers a large measure of autonomy in the scheduling of activities but little structure, no objective performance standards for either housekeeping or mothering, few opportunities for social contact, and minimal social prestige. The isolated nuclear family severely restricts social interaction with adults for full-time homemakers (Gove and Tudor 1973; Lopata 1971; Shehan 1984). However, in a study of mothers with children under 12 living in upstate New York in 1956, Miller, Moen, and Dempster-McClain (1991) found that, even in the family-oriented 1950s, the majority of homemakers (as well as employed mothers) were engaged in other social roles and that the more roles they were engaged in, the higher their psychological well-being was. Still, being a homemaker can be constraining, and in the 1950s Gavron was pointing out that "the mother at home with young children is isolated from the main stream of society" (1966:146). A study of working-class women in the 1970s, which supported this conclusion, found that 41 percent of the housewives interviewed felt they had little chance to see people during the day (Ferree 1976). A study of Boston area women conducted in the early 1980s found that housewives reporting boredom, isolation, and concern about not earning money were the most prone to psychological distress. Conversely, those seeing the domestic role as compatible with their skills were less likely to report such symptoms (Baruch 1984; Baruch, Barnett, and Rivers 1984). This suggests that, as in the case of working mothers, there are captive and committed homemakers and that captivity at home, as in employment, is consequential for women's psychological well-being.[28]

The social and psychological meaning of full-time homemaking may well change as fewer women serve exclusively and permanently as homemakers. As evidence of her lack of power or prestige, a homemaker still often describes herself as "only a housewife."[29]

Health

The relationship between employment and women's physical health is both straightforward and ambiguous. What is straightforward is the fact that employed women are typically healthier than the nonemployed, regardless of their age or the year in which they were studied (see Repetti, Matthews, and Waldron 1989; Baruch, Biener, and Barnett 1987). At every age level, employed women report fewer chronic conditions and less short- or long-term disability than do full-time homemakers. Women who are wives and mothers as well as wage earners have higher levels of physical well-being than those who do not fill any one of these roles.[30]

But are working women healthier because of their employment, or are the healthier individuals more likely to work? Both interpretations are probably true. Healthy women are active in a number of roles, including paid work. And being active promotes better health. However, some types of employment, when combined with marriage and motherhood, may be related to coronary disease. One ten-year study, for example, showed that those most vulnerable to heart disease were married mothers who had three or more children and who were employed in clerical occupations. Further adding to our understanding of the employment-health link is the finding that married women who had been employed for more than a year were healthier than those who had worked for only a short period of time (Welch and Booth 1977). To be sure, both groups were healthy enough to work. But, since those employed longer were healthier, it may be that the positive relationship typically found between employment and health does not result from healthy women choosing to work but from the effects of their work experience as well. Other studies using longitudinal data have underscored the positive effects of employment (see Waldron et al. 1982; Waldron and Jacobs 1988, 1989; Wethington and Kessler 1989; Wethington 1990).

ROLE OVERLOAD AND CONFLICT

I've teased her, although I do mean it half seriously, that if she becomes pregnant I'll quit my job, and I'll stay home and take care of the kid and write. I could see doing that. I mean, if it's anything like taking care of my cat, it's going to be a picnic (husband in dual career marriage). (Hertz 1986:134)

Caring for a new baby is a far cry from caring for a pet, and combining infant or child care with a job is infinitely more formidable. Two concepts come into play here: role *overload*, that is, bearing responsibilities whose demands exceed available time and energy resources, and role *conflict*, or the experience of confronting incompatible obligations. Investigators in the 1950s and 1960s found that working mothers were likely to doubt their adequacy as mothers, citing the inherent conflict between mothering and employment.[31]

The conflicts and overloads experienced in the 1950s continue to plague many working mothers today. A study of the transition to parenthood in the 1970s found that women who tried to combine work and family roles faced the inevitability of overload. As described by one woman:

For the first time in my life I was having to make trade-offs. To work, to have a child, to be a wife, to take care of a home, to have friends, to be a part of our new community, and to try to do all of these things well meant that something had to get cheated a little bit in each area. Not enough so that anybody else would notice, maybe, but I did. I noticed it. Sometimes I feel like my life is one long skid. Every moment I don't careen into something, I'm grateful. (Daniels and Weingarten 1982:129)

Women in professional occupations who waited to have children until their careers were established identified their jobs and not their infants as the source of strain and overload. As one woman explains:

New motherhood brought out the conflict between motherhood and work. It brought everything closer to the surface. If my job was causing me more frustration than it was giving me pleasure, why should I leave this adorable little kid? Things I would have taken at work a year or two ago, I was simply not willing to put up with any more. I guess I required a lot more satisfaction from what I was leaving the house to go do than I had before. (Daniels and Weingarten 1982:128–29)

Career-oriented women are the most likely to experience conflict between work and family roles, which suggests that such conflict occurs when a woman is absorbed in her job at the same time that she is highly invested in mothering. Indeed, work/family overload and conflict seem directly related to hours on the job. It may well be that *conflict* is more a problem of middle-class women, who have the financial means to provide for child care but who still worry about the effects of their employment on their children, while women in working-class jobs may suffer more from role *overload*, struggling to manage child-care costs and timetables on a limited budget and with little flexibility in their working hours (cf. Pearlin 1975). A 1986 national survey of 1,000 adults in households with children found that 44 percent of the mothers working more than forty hours a week were likely to report some or much work-related stress on family life, compared to just 8 percent of those working twenty hours or less per week (Opinion Research Corporation 1987; see also Hochschild 1989; Voydanoff 1988; Crosby 1987).

Work/family conflict and overload are also related, of course, to the nature of a woman's family responsibilities. Single-parent mothers, for example, are particularly vulnerable, as are mothers of very young children.[32] Still, both mothers and fathers have trouble combining work and family roles. A 1989 *New York Times* poll reported that 83 percent of working mothers and 72 percent of working fathers (with children under 18) felt torn between the demands of their jobs and their desire to spend more time with their families (Belkin 1989).

TRENDS

What can we conclude about possible trends coupling employment to women's psychological and physical well-being? Employment may have beneficial outcomes, but there are no simple time lines that chart improvements in well-being in tandem with the upturn in the number of women combining paid work with child care and housework. Rather, the connection between employment and well-being is contingent on a variety of factors in women's lives. Employment may be conducive to greater well-being, but it also can lead to role conflict and overload, especially for mothers of young children. This was the case in the 1950s when relatively few mothers of preschoolers were in the labor force, and it remains true today. Whether employment leads to beneficial or deleterious outcomes for women who are raising young children seems to depend on a complex calculus of costs and benefits. When the perceived benefits exceed the costs, the overall consequence of employment is salutary. Conversely, when the strains and overloads exceed the rewards, the outcome may be less than positive. While employment appears to be generally related to women's health, both physical and mental, the balance sheet is somewhat less favorable for employed mothers of young children than for employed women without children or for those whose children are older.

At least five considerations preclude finding any simple cause-and-effect connection between maternal employment and well-being. The first is personal preference. Until recent years, employment for many middle-class mothers of young children was more an option than a necessity. Those who found the balance sheet more heavily weighted with costs than benefits could opt to leave the labor force until family pressures lessened or better working arrangements could be found. Mothers of young children who were employed because they wished to work outside the home, rather than out of economic necessity, regarded their situations positively (i.e., the committed and the copers). The importance of personal preference for a role—be it full-time homemaker or full-time worker—cannot be overstated. Women who are reluctantly employed (the captives and the conflicted) are not likely to benefit psychologically from it. But the available evidence suggests that women today are more likely to be committed to their employment than captive to it, although they may wish for fewer hours on the job.

The second consideration involves the nature of the relationship between multiple roles and well-being. Is it role accumulation—having a number of roles—or, more specifically, the employment role that produces a given outcome? One way of answering this question is to look at individuals who are employed but are neither married nor mothers. In examining national health statistics (Health Interview Survey), it is clear that women who are divorced or separated have higher rates of acute and chronic ailments than do married women, regardless of their employment status. Moreover, women with children at home are typically healthier than childless women, again regardless of employment. The evidence suggests, at least in the case of physical health, that employment, marriage, and parenting are all positively related to physical health although the causal direction (whether these roles contribute to health or reflect existing health) remains problematic. But, since more women are now employed, this suggests at least a gradual improvement in women's well-being over time.

> The more roles women have, the better their health. Women with few roles have poorest health. Women with three major roles (employment, marriage, parenthood) tend to have the best health status and to engage in fewest curative actions. Both selection and causation are factors: only the healthiest women can manage several roles. On the other hand, multiple roles give women several sources of satisfaction and achievement. (Verbrugge 1982:265)

The salutary effects of multiple role involvements, not just employment per se, have been established for women in the 1970s and 1980s as well as in the 1950s (Miller, Moen, Dempster-McClain 1991; Moen, Dempster-McClain, and Williams 1989, 1992; Thoits 1983, 1986).

The third consideration, which ties together the two previous considerations, concerns the degree to which satisfaction in the performance of one role can compensate for dissatisfaction in another. Does being happy in one's job make up for deficits in one's marriage or family life, or vice versa? Researchers have yet to answer this question satisfactorily, although there seems to be more evidence of spillover from one role to another than evidence of compensation.[33]

Fourth, we must take into account the specific contexts of both work and the family in any assessment of psychological or physical health effects. The more easily employment can be integrated with family responsibilities, the less likely are negative consequences. Here we must consider, among other things, the nature of the work performed and the flexibility of the job, the number and ages of the children, and the presence (and helpfulness) of a spouse—not merely whether or not a woman is employed. For example, part-time work appears to have more salutary consequences for the psychological well-being of mothers of young children. Similarly, the evidence suggests that having fewer children should reduce the overloads on working mothers. However, the increasing number of single parents means that, for many women, the strains of combining work and family roles have become especially acute.

Finally, we must consider the possibility that the effects of employment on women's physical and mental health have changed in conjunction with the progressive transformations that have occurred in society's attitudes about gender roles. Indeed, an analysis of data from a number of surveys conducted from 1957 to 1976 led Kessler and McRae (1981, 1982) to conclude not only that employment has positive outcomes for women generally but also that its benefits have increased over the years.[34]

It may well be that maternal employment in the United States in the 1990s is more beneficial to women's emotional health than ever before, despite the role conflicts and overloads it inevitably introduces. Studies conducted in the 1950s, 1960s, and early 1970s, when such employment was less common than today, found widespread feelings of guilt and anxiety among working mothers (Nye 1974a). Now that maternal employment is more the rule rather than the exception, the prevalence and level of guilt may well have lessened. Still, given the structural lags in the organization of work and their double burden at home and at work, women continue to experience role overloads and conflicts. But many see their employment as beneficial, both to themselves and to their families. One sociologist describes the traditional attitude of women as "if the family does well, I do too" (Scanzoni 1978:116). But growing numbers of employed mothers may be adopting the orientation characteristic of men in our society: "If I do well, the family does too."

NOTES

1. The life course perspective, which adopts a dynamic approach, examines trajectories and transitions in roles and relationships throughout life. It also places these trajectories and transitions in historical and cultural contexts; the life course of women at the turn of the century, for example, is vastly different from the life course of women today, and being a working mother in Sweden is far different from being a working mother in the United States. See Elder (1975, 1985), Clausen (1986), and Moen (1989).

2. Several studies point to the importance of children (Waite 1980; Cain 1966; Sweet 1973; Felmlee 1984; Presser and Baldwin 1980; Cramer 1980; Moen 1985; Moore and Hofferth 1979; Sorensen 1983).

3. See Gordon and Kammeyer (1980) and Waite, Haggstrom, and Kanouse (1985).

4. See Berk (1985), Moen, (1985), and Wethington and Kessler (1989).

5. Between 1940 and 1970, almost 40 percent of the increase in the number of employed women occurred in part-time work (Leon and Bednarzik 1978). In fact, the majority of adults working part-time have been, and continue to be, women, and the best predictors of part-time hours are being married and having young (or many) children (Barrett 1979; Belous 1989; Kahne 1985; Nine to Five 1986; Leon and Bednarzik 1978; Moen and Dempster-McClain 1987).

6. See Ferree (1987) for a discussion of working-class women. For part-time employment as a means of maintaining an attachment to work, see Yohalem (1979), Moen and Smith (1986), Kahne (1985), and Moen (1989).

7. See Presser (1986, 1987, 1988, 1989), and Presser and Cain (1983). Data from the Current Population Survey from 1958 to 1982 reveal that this strategy has been used frequently by working parents over the years (U.S. Bureau of the Census 1982, 1983).

8. For an understanding of the plight of single-parent mothers, see Garfinkel and McLanahan (1986) and Weitzman (1985).

9. Moreover, the declining fertility rate is producing consternation among some concerned with population replacement and distribution (e.g., Wattenberg 1987).

10. See Angrist and Almquist (1975), Gerson (1985), Hertz (1986), Rossi (1965), Yohalem (1979), Waite and Stolzenberg (1976), and Waite (1980).

11. Closely allied to these preferences are attitudes about roles. A large majority (67.6%) of employed women in the Detroit study liked their jobs; only 45 percent of the homemakers liked their homemaking chores.

12. See Felmlee (1984). See also Waite and Stolzenberg (1976) for the effects of beliefs about the impact on children on women's employment.

13. See also Moen and Smith (1986) and Bielby and Bielby (1989). A recent study has found that women with low work commitment are more influenced by financial pressures and job characteristics in making decisions about leaving the labor force following the birth of their first child (Desai, Leibowitz, and Waite 1989).

14. Several studies are relevant here: Cleary and Mechanic (1983), Gove (1972), Gove and Tudor (1973), Kessler and McRae (1982), Menaghan (1989), Moen (1989), Moen and Forest (1990), Radloff (1975), and Reskin and Coverman (1985).

15. This difference in labor force attachment remains true in the 1990s, even though the gender gap has been continuously narrowing.

16. There is considerable support for this viewpoint: Andrews and Withey (1976), Brown and Harris (1978), Gove (1972), Gove and Hughes (1979), Pearlin (1975), McLanahan and Adams (1987), and Menaghan (1989). However, Wethington and Kessler (1989) did not find that the birth of additional children was associated with any increase in psychological distress.

17. Research has underscored this isolation (Bernard 1972; Gove and Tudor 1973; Gove 1972; Shehan 1984).

18. The following social scientists are associated with this view: Sieber (1974), Marks (1977), Thoits (1983, 1986), Barnett and Baruch (1985).

19. Such strain is seen as a perceived difficulty in meeting role obligations (Goode 1960; Coser and Rokoff 1971; Pearlin 1975; Burr et al. 1979:78).

20. Studies of role conflict and strain include those by Hall (1972), Herman and Gyllstrom (1977), and Kandel, Davies, and Raveis (1985).

21. Some studies find positive effects (Baruch, Biener, and Barnett 1987; Bernard 1972; Gore and Mangione 1983; Roberts, Roberts, and Stevenson 1982; Kessler and McRae 1982; Gove and Geerken 1977; Gove and Tudor 1973; Thoits 1986; Welch and Booth 1977; Wethington and Kessler 1989; Wethington 1990). For negative outcomes, see Feld 1963; Cleary and Mechanic 1983; Northcutt 1981; Pearlin 1975; Radloff 1975. Others find little difference (Rosenfield 1980; Aneshensel, Frerichs, and Clark 1981). See also the review by Mirowsky and Ross (1986) and the analysis by Rosenfield (1989).

22. See Gove and Peterson (1980), Scanzoni and Fox (1980), Kessler and McRae (1981), Pearlin (1975), Warr and Parry (1982), Campbell (1982), and Faver (1984).

23. See Krause (1984) and Ross, Mirowsky, and Huber (1983).

24. See Kessler and McRae (1982), as well as Rapoport and Rapoport (1976) and Ross, Mirowsky, and Huber (1983). Other potentially important factors affecting the ties between work and well-being may be interpersonal relationships, both on and off the job; however, the influence of relationships—with husbands, children, bosses, and coworkers—has yet to be clearly established (Long and Porter 1984:120).

25. One study, however, using data collected between 1959 and 1962, did find that employment had a positive effect on the psychological well-being of both black and white women when social class was taken into consideration (Reskin and Coverman 1985). On the other hand, studies of Mexican American women have yielded contradictory findings; some report positive results (Ross, Mirowsky, and Ulbrich 1983), and others report mixed results (Krause and Markides 1987).

26. There are a number of important studies (Cleary and Mechanic 1983; Cohen et al. 1990; Crouter 1984; Emmons et al. 1990; Warr and Parry 1982; Rosenfield 1989; Holahan and Gilbert 1979; Aneshensel, Frerichs, and Clark 1981; Voydanoff 1988) and reviews (McLanahan and Adams 1987; Repetti, Matthews, and Waldron 1989) on this topic.

27. See Gove and Geerken (1977), Radloff (1975), Gore and Mangione (1983), Ross, Mirowsky, and Ulbrich (1983), and Shehan (1984). One national survey, conducted in 1976, found that the positive effects of employment were much weaker for mothers than for women without children in the home (Campbell 1982).

28. Komarovsky's research on working-class marriages in the 1950s concluded that women with less than a high school education were happier in the role of homemaker than were those with more education (Komarovsky 1962). This conclusion was supported by Ferree (1976) who found that working-class housewives were happier than middle-class housewives.

29. See Komarovsky (1953) and Lopata (1971).

30. Data are taken from the national Health Interview Survey. See Verbrugge (1982, 1983, 1985, 1987). See also Nye (1974a), Sharp and Nye (1963), Feld (1963), Northcutt (1981), Welch and Booth (1974, 1977), Woods and Hulka (1979), Haynes and Feinleib (1980), and Nathanson (1980).

31. See Feld (1963) and Nye (1974a). For a discussion of overload and conflict, see Rapoport and Rapoport (1965, 1975, 1976).

32. The presence, age, and number of children all contribute to work/family tensions. Studies confirm the common experience of role conflict among employed mothers of young children and the special problems of single-parent families (Cohen et al. 1990; Emmons et al. 1990; Holahan and Gilbert 1979; Rapoport and Rapoport 1976; Campbell and Moen 1992; Kelly and Voydanoff 1985; Voydanoff and Kelly 1984; McLanahan and Adams 1987).

33. Several studies touch on this situation: Baruch, Biener, and Barnett (1987), Downey and Moen (1987), Radloff (1975), Long and Porter (1984), and Spreitzer, Snyder, and Larson (1975, 1979). More micro analyses of spillover are reported in Bolger et al. (1989), and a fuller discussion of the boundaries between work and family roles is provided by Eckenrode and Gore (1990).

34. An analysis of data from two surveys, one in each of these years, shows an improvement in the proportions of both employed and nonemployed mothers of young children reporting positive self-perceptions.

4 IMPLICATIONS FOR MARRIAGES, FAMILIES, AND CHILDREN

> Of all the rationales offered for women's presence in the home, the myth of motherhood seems the most persuasive and the least questionable in its premises and conclusions, for even if the housewife role and the wife role are capable of change, the maternal role is not.
>
> *(Oakley 1974:186)*

Family life in the United States has changed markedly throughout this century, but most dramatically so since the baby boom years of the 1950s. Young people increasingly postpone marriage; a small but growing number forgo it altogether. Similarly, more couples now delay childbearing and give birth to fewer children. They are also more likely to divorce, which, in conjunction with an acceleration in the proportion of births outside marriage, has led to a substantial growth in the number of single-parent families. Residential mobility has been a long-term trend, with families both moving to the suburbs and relocating to communities promising greater economic growth and employment opportunities. And there has been a progressive trend toward gender equality, as evidenced by the narrowing of the gap between men and women in educational achievement. Within this constellation of change, the expanding number of employed mothers of young children has had a particularly broad and strong impact on family life.

THE CHANGING SHAPE OF MARRIAGE

Women increasingly want to have it both ways: a happy home life and a successful career. But for most employed mothers, having it both ways means having two jobs: one at home and one at work, with little help on the home front. The relationships between men and women in society are being redefined, but the relationships between husbands and wives are slow to change. This points to the transitional nature of this revolution in gender roles, with men and women holding ambiguous and often conflicting expectations for themselves and for their spouses. For example, the belief that the husband should be the principal occupational achiever remained deeply rooted into the 1970s, as expressed by the college men interviewed in an in-depth study conducted by sociologist Mirra Komarovsky (1976). These men paid lip service to the principle of equality, asserting that mothers of preschoolers should be able to take full-time jobs, "provided, of course, that the home was running smoothly, the children did not suffer and the wife did not interfere with her husband's career." In fact, the most common attitude among these college men can be described as that of a "modified traditionalist," advocating the sequential pattern of women's employment, i.e., leaving their jobs for child rearing and then returning to work when their children are school age. Komarovksy's findings are consistent with those of large-scale surveys of nationally representative samples of men. As documented in Chapter 2, even in the mid-1980s, most men believed there could be no substitute for a mother's care during the preschool years. A major portion (62.7%) of men interviewed in 1985, regardless of educational level, agreed that a pre-school child is likely to suffer if his or her mother works.[1]

Ambivalent—even contradictory—values, ideologies, and personal preferences appear to be deeply entrenched: "It is only fair to let a woman do her own thing, if she wants a career. Personally, though, I would want my wife at home" (Komarovsky 1976, p. 34). These internal conflicts reflect in some ways what some observers see as an inherent clash between the goals of women's equality and of family well-being. Historian Carl Degler sees these as being "at odds" with one another (1980), and George Gilder describes women's growing equality as "catastrophic" to the emotional health of men in our society (1986). Is the employment of wives truly a "catastrophe" for husbands? Or, to the contrary, might men actually benefit from it? These questions cannot be answered without first addressing another issue: continuity and change in the division of family work—housework and child care—between husbands and wives.

The Division of Labor

Women may have come a long way in terms of employment and gender-role attitudes, but the fact remains that, whether or not employed, they continue to perform by far the greatest share of family work. This has been a consistent finding throughout nearly thirty years of research.[2]

Some scholars explain the persistence of this traditional division of labor in terms of "resource theory"—husbands and fathers simply do not have the time to devote to domestic activity, given their heavy involvement in occupations (Blood and Wolfe 1960). Others see it as a "system of exchange"—men provide the family with income and social status, and their wives in turn assume the burden of domestic chores (Scanzoni 1970, 1978). This second perspective is closely in tune with the "new home economics" approach of economist Gary Becker, who suggests that the traditional division of labor makes sense as a means of maximizing household "utility" (Becker 1981; Berk and Berk 1983).

But if wives are also working, if they also are bringing home a paycheck, what then? Both these interpretations imply a trend toward more equitable sharing of domestic work as wives and mothers themselves face the time constraints of employment and gain status and income from their work.

In contrast, the feminist perspective says that women's heavy domestic load is a consequence of patriarchy, the domination of women by men in all sectors of society. According to this view, gender roles within the household are deeply embedded within the larger system of social relations; employment may increase women's economic resources and even improve their self-esteem, but it will not lighten their burden at home (Hartmann 1981; Sokoloff 1980, 1988; Walby 1986).

Time-use data collected in the 1960s and early 1970s revealed that a husband's contribution to domestic work was unrelated to whether his wife was employed. However, by the late 1970s, men with employed wives did spend more time each week in housework and child care than did husbands who were sole breadwinners.[3] This trend over the 1970s decade may represent a significant shift in men's and women's roles, especially since the family work of husbands with wives who are *not* employed has also increased over the years. But it is important to note that husbands typically "help" their wives rather than assume a major responsibility for particular household tasks (Geerken and Gove 1983; Pleck 1985, 1986).

Consider, for example, the greater involvement of fathers in child care when their wives are employed. Typically their participation is limited to playing with the children or to caring for them when their wives are not present. Still, the fact that fathers of young children are spending more time in child care does suggest at least the beginnings of a convergence in the domestic responsibilities of men and women.[4]

Figure 4.1
Trends in Average Time Spent on Housework by Mothers and Fathers of Preschoolers, 1965–1985

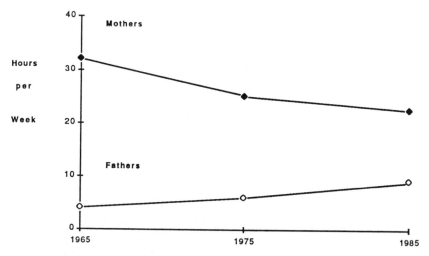

Source: Adapted from Robinson 1988: 27.

Note: Housework includes cooking, meal cleanup, housecleaning, laundry and ironing, outdoor chores, home repairs, garden and pet care, and paying bills and other managerial tasks.

This convergence can also be seen in the changes occurring in the amount of time devoted to housework, as women spend less time in household work (as a result of their smaller families and increased employment) and men spend slightly more. In 1965 married women did more than five times as much housework as did married men, but by 1985 they did only twice as much. Figure 4.1 illustrates the trends from 1965 to 1985 in the average hours per week spent in housework by parents of preschoolers, with mothers cutting their time in housework by almost one third and fathers more than doubling their housework hours. Beyond doubt this is a remarkable change.

The principal factors that seem to influence the division of household work between spouses are as follows:

- Husband's income—the higher his income, the less likely he is to share in domestic work.

- Wife's earnings—the more she earns, the more her husband is involved with housework.

- Presence of children—having young children increases the likelihood of a husband's domestic involvement.
- Wife's education—the greater the wife's education, the greater the husband's involvement, at least in some tasks.
- Husband's education—the higher the husband's level of education, the greater his share of the housework.
- Husband's work hours—the more hours the husband spends on the job, the less his involvement in housework and child care.[5]

These effects of husbands' and wives' education and the presence of preschoolers may be changing over time, with younger cohorts of husbands more influenced by these factors than older cohorts. The influence of another variable, race, may also be changing. Studies in the early 1970s found that black husbands did more work around the home than white husbands. However, race has not been a significant predictor of housework in later studies.[6]

The last half of the 1970s may have been a real turning point in the distribution of housework between husbands and wives. Where change particularly appears to have occurred is among fathers of young children. These fathers in the late 1970s and 1980s appeared to be more involved in the family's domestic work than ever before, *regardless* of whether their wives were employed.[7]

But there is more to housework and child care than meets the eye. Men may be putting in time around the house, but women remain burdened with the principal *responsibility* for family life. As Robert and Rhona Rapoport noted in their study of professional couples in Great Britain in the 1960s:

It is the wife who must remember about things that have to be done in the home, even though they may have negotiated an agreement to share responsibilities. The husband simply forgets once he has left the house, wiping his mind clean of domestic concerns because he has been programmed by society to shift his attention to external concerns. (1976:368)

In fact, economist Heidi Hartmann (1981) suggests that the care and feeding of *husbands* may require more household work than they themselves contribute.[8]

Social psychologists Joseph Pleck and Michael Lamb and their colleagues specify four factors that should influence the involvement of fathers in the care of their young children: motivation, skills, social supports, and the absence of institutional barriers.[9] "Institutional barriers" include the ways in which jobs are structured, leaving little time available for child care. These barriers are central to the feminist perspective, which underscores the fact that women's domestic work frees men to devote full time to their jobs, emotionally as well as physically. This view suggests that the division of household work cannot become truly equitable until basic changes are made in the workplace, erasing the myth of the unencumbered (male) worker.

Division of Power

Some social scientists explain men's power in conventional marriages in exchange terms: Husbands provide the income and status and, thereby, "earn" an entitlement to be the principal decision makers. According to this perspective, wives' employment, which increases their resources and options, should produce a greater equity in household decision making. Studies over the years have, in fact, affirmed the relationship between wives' earning power and their power in the marriage. Working-class wives in particular seem to gain the most from employment, possibly since their earnings are so critical to the family economy.[10]

Feminist scholars locate the source of the power inequity between husbands and wives in the larger system of patriarchy and its ideology of male dominance. The exploitation of women at home and at work, they argue, augers to the benefit of men. Accordingly, it is not apt to disappear easily, regardless of the recent trends in women's employment. Indeed, from a feminist perspective, women's roles, resources, and relationships both at home and in the workplace serve to perpetuate gender inequalities (Reskin 1988; Sokoloff 1980, 1988).

The research evidence suggests that, although employment appears to increase a wife's power in family decision making, equality of power between husbands and wives has yet to be realized. Given the ways in which women typically accommodate their jobs to their family obligations, along with persistent occupational segregation and gender discrimination, the fact is that wives seldom approach their husbands in earnings capacity. In most cases the financial resources they bring to the marriage merely supplement the income earned by their husbands. The lives of husbands and wives remain seriously constrained by gender expectations. Thus, the division of power between husbands and wives, like the division of household work, remains markedly skewed, but in the opposite direction.

Implications for the Marital Relationship

Each marriage bears the footprints of economic and cultural trends which originate far outside marriage. (Hochschild 1989:11)

Social scientists address the effects of a wife's employment on the quality of marriage from several viewpoints. One postulates a positive outcome: Dual-earner couples should have more in common since they share the wage-earning (and may come to share the homemaking) role. This view builds on a long sociological tradition associating role sharing with the warmth of relationships between spouses.[11]

But others predict negative outcomes. These scholars feel that the traditional division of labor between spouses may well be the most effective way of managing the multiple demands of family life. Accordingly, a "working" wife may mean competition between husband and wife, or, at the very least, the working wife and mother may disrupt her husband's and children's lives by failing to do all that needs to be done at home.[12]

Are husbands and wives less satisfied with their marriages when both spouses work? To answer that question we have to consider the evolution of women's roles over time. Married women's employment might have been problematic for marriage during the 1950s when it was considered somewhat deviant, but the social climate has changed. Early research on that topic did, in fact, find less marital satisfaction among dual-employed couples than among those in which the wife was a full-time homemaker. But, by the late 1960s and early 1970s, this difference had disappeared (Axelson 1963; Feld 1963; Nye 1974b).

A major survey of couples conducted in the late 1960s by Susan Orden and Norman Bradburn (1969) illuminated the issue by looking at both marital satisfactions and tensions—recognizing that they are not the same thing—and by separating out employed women who *wanted* to work from those who preferred to be homemakers (contrast committed and captive women). They found that employed women who did not want to be in the labor force, those captive to the work role, had both much tension and little satisfaction in their marriages. Moreover, these researchers discovered an important life-cycle difference. When preschoolers were in the home, both husbands and wives evaluated their marriages more positively when the wives were not in the labor force. Employed wives who were committed to the work role and whose children were school age were the most positive in describing their marriages, as were their husbands. For parents of high schoolers, however, the wife's employment made little difference in marital satisfaction.

More recent investigations highlight the importance of gender-role attitudes—especially those of the husband—in moderating the links between the wife's employment and both spouses' marital satisfaction. When husbands are more egalitarian in their attitudes and values, they report a higher quality marriage, regardless of whether their wives are employed. Similarly, employed wives report higher levels of marital satisfaction when their husbands are more supportive and share in the care of children (Philliber and Hiller 1983; Kessler and McRae 1982).

There is evidence also that the *nature* as well as the mere fact of the wife's employment must be taken into account. Two studies conducted in the early 1960s found that part-time women workers had higher levels of marital satisfaction than full-time workers. And recent studies suggest that the conditions of work for both parents must be considered, with stress on the job associated with marital conflict and strain.[13]

What may be critical too is a wife's status and earnings *relative to those of her husband*. Men whose wives are more successful than they are may be particularly dissatisfied with their marriages. But the evidence on this issue is still ambiguous.[14]

Historical trends concerning the effects of a wife's employment on her (or her husband's) marital satisfaction are by no means clear from the evidence on hand. Some surveys report no difference in levels of marital satisfaction as a function of the wife's employment; others find husbands of employed wives less satisfied with their marriages than single-earner husbands.[15]

But what do we mean by "marital satisfaction"? Studies use various measures of marital adjustment, ranging from reported happiness, conflict, and satisfaction to joint recreational activities and the absence of negative comments about the spouse. Different findings may be a result of different measures used. There is also the problem of "selection bias": The unhappiest couples are not studied because they have probably already been divorced! In fact, wives who work are more likely than full-time homemakers to divorce their husbands. Marriages bonded only by financial dependency are less likely to continue once wives attain some degree of economic independence through employment (Booth, Johnson, and Whyte 1984; Cherlin 1981).

This suggests that the trend in women's employment may have a positive impact on the quality of marriages, since fewer women will either enter into or remain in marriages simply for financial reasons. When both spouses work, the marriage benefits in terms of more income but suffers in terms of the availability and flexibility of time. And couple decisions—whether to move, when to have a child—become more complicated when two jobs are involved. Most likely a wife's employment follows various pathways in affecting her marriage: altering how she sees herself, the time she has for and the demands placed upon the marital relationship, her (and their) resources, and how her husband sees himself. Whether the wife's employment is good (or bad) for the husband and, by connotation, for the marriage depends, as we shall see below, on how the husband feels about his wife's being employed.

Implications for Husbands' Well-Being

Some studies indicate that wives' employment may have deleterious effects on the mental health of their husbands. Trend data are admittedly sparse; the earliest study, based on only thirty married couples in 1965, reported higher levels of depression among husbands with employed wives (Rosenfield 1980). In addition, data from a 1976 survey of a large, nationally representative sample, analyzed by sociologists Ronald Kessler and James McRae (1982), reveal an association between wives' employment and depression and low self-esteem among husbands. These relationships persist even after taking into account the husbands' ages and incomes as well as the number and ages of children. Kessler and McRae tested for the possibility of role overload by including in their analysis whether or not the husbands of employed wives frequently do housework or are involved in child care. However, these family chores were found not to be related to the psychological distress of husbands— with one small exception. Fathers with working wives who did *not* assist in child care were *more* likely to report ill health and psychological anxiety than those participating in caretaking.[16]

Another analysis of these data, which tested the effects of wives' incomes (both absolute level and as a proportion of total family income) on husbands' well-being, found that husbands' improved mental health goes hand in hand with increases in their wives' incomes. This suggests that it is something other than the loss of status and power as the sole breadwinner that produces mental distress in the husbands of employed wives.

Kessler and McRae also discovered that the negative effects of a wife's employment are greatest in mid-life; young husbands and husbands approaching retirement are less likely to show mental distress in conjunction with their wives' employment. They suggest that this finding may reflect both age and cohort effects. Older men may have accommodated to the situation (age effect); younger men may be more liberal regarding women's roles (cohort effect). Thus, at least part of the negative impact of a wife's employment on her husband's well-being should diminish with the passage of time, as younger cohorts replace older ones, because younger couples are more accepting of this new life-style.

Missing in the Kessler and McRae study is any measure of the husband's attitudes toward sex roles in general and toward his own wife's employment in particular. This gap is filled in another nationwide survey of couples conducted in 1978. In this study Catherine Ross, John Mirowsky, and Joan Huber (1983) found that the deleterious effects of a wife's employment are greatly increased if the husband does not *want* his wife to be employed. Conversely, men who supported their wives' employment reported the lowest depression levels. As in the earlier study conducted by Kessler and McRae, this research found that neither the wife's earnings nor the husband's involvement in housework had any effect on the husband's depression. A husband's preference for his wife to be employed was negatively correlated with age; that is, younger men were more apt than older ones to approve of their wives' employment. This again suggests that future cohorts of husbands may find having a working wife less problematic than has been true in the past.

Other studies suggest that characteristics of the wife's job may affect the husband's well-being. For example, having a wife who works part-time has been shown to have a salutary effect on her husband's psychological health.[17]

Historical trend data on the well-being of husbands can be considered on two levels. First, husbands of employed wives generally have been psychologically worse off than husbands with wives who were home-makers. Second, this effect may be disappearing as new cohorts of younger husbands accept and even endorse the employment of their wives.

TRADING TIME FOR MONEY

The institutions of the society make no allowances for alternative conceptions of time. They impose rigid and standard time schedules on all. (Harriman 1982:4)

Time has become the new scarcity in American families. As a fixed commodity, the time allocated to employment is necessarily unavailable for other activities, including family affairs. When mothers of young children combine domestic work with paid work, their families gain in income and the women themselves may gain in self-esteem. What is *lost* is time—for the couples, for the families, and for the women themselves. Time constraints in working families are experienced disproportionately by women, and these constraints are especially problematic for single-parent mothers.

Time pressures necessarily limit the number of joint activities working parents can undertake—with their children and with each other. The competition for time between work and family is seldom resolved; rather, obligations to both are juggled in a time-budgeting process that is often unsatisfactory for both parents and their children.

The early years of childbearing are especially demanding. Infants and preschoolers not only take more time, but they also impose demands that cannot fit into a rigid, predetermined schedule.[18] Sociologist John Robinson, examining time use in a 1973 national survey, found that, "other factors being equal, a child under four years of age received 50 percent more of a mother's contact time and three times as much of her primary activity time than a comparable child beyond the preschool age of four" (1977:80).

Working mothers with jobs have more to do than those who do not work outside the home, but they spend less time on housework.[19] Moreover women generally, whether employed or not, are spending less and less time on housework, as time-use studies show. In fact, from 1965 to 1985, the amount of time spent on household tasks decreased more sharply for *nonemployed* women (ten–hour per week drop) than for employed women (three–hour per week drop). These trends are illustrated in Figure 4.2.

Still, women with paid jobs put in fewer hours on domestic chores than do full-time homemakers. Housework is somewhat elastic—expanding to fill open hours and contracting when time is scarce. This explains why employed women spent on average 41 percent less time in housework than did nonemployed women in 1965. It also explains why women in the 1960s spent as much time doing housework as did women in the 1920s to 1950s, despite the advances in household technology.

But today women are having fewer children and hold less exacting housekeeping standards—hence the reduction in time spent on domestic chores. There have been societal adjustments as well: the burgeoning number of restaurants and fast-food chains, microwave dinners, and take-out meals available in grocery stores and delis, for example, along with the proliferation of vendored services such as housecleaning and child care. But raising children is not nearly so flexible as housework. Parents, especially mothers, "invest" in their children; they assume that

Figure 4.2

Trends in Average Time Spent on Housework by Men and Women Aged 18 to 65, by Employment Status, 1965–1985

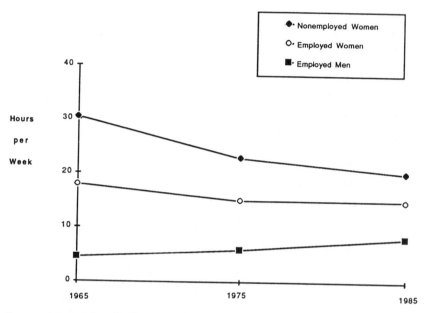

Source: Adapted from Robinson 1988: 28.

Note: Housework includes cooking, meal cleanup, housecleaning, laundry and ironing, outdoor chores, home repairs, garden and pet care, and paying bills and other managerial tasks.

the more quality time they spend with their children, the better their development will be. Thus, it should come as no surprise that employed single-parent mothers spend *less* time in household chores than do those who are not employed, but the *same* amount of time in child care.

Economists Russell Hill and Frank Stafford (1974, 1980) report that college-educated women give up sleep in order to care for their children and that the amount of time these women spend with their children does not diminish with their employment. But Barbara Willer (1986), drawing on data from the 1977 Quality of Employment Survey, found that employed mothers of preschoolers with higher income levels spent less time with their children than did those with lower incomes. This finding suggests that women may, in fact, make trade-offs between income and family time. Nevertheless, with the hours spent on the job, in housework, and in child care, employed mothers of young children put in, on average, an eighty–hour week in the 1970s; fathers in such families spent only sixty-five hours overall. Trends in time use by men and women may well be converging, but they are converging at a very modest pace.[20]

Family Payoffs

The paychecks of single-parent women are crucial to supporting their families. Working wives also make a significant contribution to the economic security and well-being of their families. In 1986 wives' earnings represented about one-fourth of total family income, and wives working full-time and year-round contributed nearly 40 percent, roughly the same proportion (39%) as in 1977 (Hayghe 1978; U.S. Bureau of the Census 1986).

But the extent to which the earnings potential of women can be realized is determined by a host of cultural and institutional factors, including employment opportunities, prevailing wage rates, and the "costs" of employment. For many mothers of preschoolers, the expense and the complexity of arranging for child care makes full-time employment impossible. Single-parent mothers in particular tend to hold unstable or low-paying jobs, often in tandem with low, erratic, or even no child support payments from their children's fathers (Garfinkel and McLanahan 1986; Weitzman 1985).

The escalating costs of raising a family, in conjunction with the rise in the incidence of single-parent families, make the employment of mothers of young children increasingly consequential. Even when it is not essential to put bread on the table, the employment of wives and mothers provides a financial cushion for the family economy, as well as the wherewithal to achieve a better quality of life. In fact, one-fourth of the mothers in two-earner families surveyed in 1986 said they were working to enable the family to enjoy a higher standard of living. Not surprisingly, blue-collar workers and those with lower levels of household income were more likely to describe their reason for working as "economic necessity."[21]

An additional benefit of maternal employment to families is the mother's higher morale. Both professional and blue-collar women workers report greater happiness and satisfaction than full-time homemakers in studies conducted throughout the 1970s and 1980s. As one woman reported, "I'm nicer to my family when I get out of the house. I'm more independent, satisfied, and happier at home."[22] This sense of satisfaction, however, has been found to be contingent on women's preference for employment. The committed benefit the most; the captives benefit not at all. Moreover, the actual conditions of employment also affect a woman's sense of well-being. And, as we have seen in Chapter 3, women can be satisfied with working yet still endure role strains and overloads.

Family Costs

About one-third of the workers interviewed in a 1977 national survey reported experiencing "work-family interference," typically related to time constraints (Moen and Dempster-McClain 1987). Nine years later, in a 1986 survey, little had changed; 30 percent of the employed parents reported that their work put stress on their family lives. More wives than husbands reported not having enough time to spend with children and spouses because of work, and both husbands and wives in two-earner families experienced more time pressures than did husbands in traditional one-earner situations or single-parent women (Opinion Research Corporation 1987).

Analysis of data from the 1977 survey underscored the relationship between work/family strains and preferred work/time involvement. Mothers (and fathers) who reported such strains were five times more likely to prefer spending less time working. The 1986 survey found that those parents experiencing work/family strains were the least likely to describe their families as open in communicating with each other, close knit, basically happy, mutually helpful, or supportive. Again, the full-time women workers under strain in meshing their work and family responsibilities may well be the captive and conflicted workers—on the job but wishing they were working less or not at all at this stage of their lives when their children are young. Part of their strain can be attributed to the glacial pace of institutional change. Mothers increasingly work outside the home, but they have little opportunity to reduce their hours temporarily as necessary or to take an extended leave of absence. Neither are there enough quality, affordable, and accessible child-care arrangements available to working families.

Work/family strain is not the special province of women. A 1989 *New York Times* survey of mothers and fathers with children under age 18 found that 83 percent of the mothers and 72 percent of the fathers felt torn between the demands of their jobs and wanting to spend more time with their families at least sometimes. About one-third of both men and women respondents felt that children and family life suffered most when a woman tries to combine a job, marriage, and children (Cowan 1989).

Marriage. The amount of time working couples spend in employment is typically "negotiated" between spouses as a trade-off between family time and financial needs. These decisions are made against a backdrop of deeply embedded cultural expectations. One such expectation is that fathers should work at least a forty–hour week. But mothers also are commonly locked into jobs where standard hours are prescribed, regardless of family needs. Both the number of hours worked and their scheduling necessarily determine the amount of time husbands and wives spend together and with their children. Shift work, for example, permits some parents to share in the care of their children. On the other hand, work in the evening and at night may exacerbate scheduling difficulties for husbands and wives.[23]

In the end, having both spouses work—regardless of their work schedules—typically means that couples spend less time together eating meals, watching television, socializing, engaging in sports, and entertaining. This limitation on "togetherness" frequently has deleterious effects on the quality of the marriage (Kingston and Nock 1987; Booth, Johnson, and Whyte 1984).

Children. Despite women's best intentions, the inevitable outcome of maternal employment is some reduction in the amount of time children spend with their mothers. There are three dimensions to the "time with children" issue.

The first is simply the *number of hours* in a day or week children spend with their mothers. Some might argue that children of employed mothers do not lose on this count because (1) working mothers, especially those with young children, may work less than a standard forty–hour week when it is financially feasible; (2) mothers may forgo other activities in their lives (such as sleep and personal care) to compensate for their hours on the job; and (3) children may be kept up later at night or awakened earlier in the morning in order to spend as much time as possible with their mothers.

Second, children may lose hours spent with their mothers, but what is lost in *quantity* may be well surpassed by the *quality* of the time mothers devote to their children. And third, children may also benefit from spending *additional time with their fathers*.

The evidence bearing on these three possibilities is ambiguous, partly because different investigators employ quite different methods, ranging from merely asking parents for rough time estimates to having them keep detailed time-use diaries. Moreover, "time with children" can mean one-on-one togetherness or simply occupying the same room at the same time. And "children" in one study may be defined as those under age 6, while in another study it includes all those under age 20. But after collating the findings from a variety of studies with a range of coding methods, definitions, and samples, the following trends seem to emerge:

1. Employed mothers do in fact spend less time in all types of activities with their children than do full-time homemakers. The greatest difference (after taking into account socioeconomic status, income, race, and parents' ages) is, not surprisingly, in the time spent with preschoolers during the work week. Working mothers of young children spend fewer minutes per day with their children in play, education, child care, "fun" activities, homemaking, and meals. This is also true of working mothers of school-age children, although the contrast with full-time homemakers in this case is not as striking.

2. Differences between working and stay-at-home mothers in the amount of time they spend with their children depend on the activity considered. For example, time spent talking with preschool children or in watching television with them does *not* vary by the mother's employment status. The largest difference, again not surprisingly, is in being with children while doing household chores. The two groups of mothers differ by only about a half-hour in time spent actually caring for children during the work week. Thus, it might appear that the quality time between mothers and preschoolers is not sacrificed when mothers are in the labor force, but "quality" is in the eye of the beholder and is very difficult to gauge in any objective fashion.

3. Fathers in dual-earner families tend to spend *less* time per workday with their children than do fathers who are traditional, single-earners. Clearly, fathers do not compensate in any major way for their wives' absence from the home. In fact, the only activity in which the husbands of employed wives seem consistently to engage in more with their children than do single-earner husbands is television watching on Sundays! However, fathers of *preschoolers* tend to spend more time with their children while their wives are away at work. This is especially true when wives work in the evening or at night or when the fathers themselves are on night or evening shifts (Presser 1986, 1989; Hoffman 1989).

THE CHANGING SHAPE OF CHILD CARE

When I worked in a sewing factory, I left work at 3:00 to pick up the kids from school and bring them home. Then I went back to work. The older child took care of the younger ones. This made me worry all the time about them and it wasn't good for the kids. (Parent testifying in hearings conducted by New York State Commission on Child Care, 1986)

In 1940, 85 percent of preschool children lived with two parents, one of whom, almost always the mother, was not in the labor force. By 1988 only 37 percent were in that situation (see again Figure 2.9). In 1940 only 8 percent of preschoolers had both parents (or their sole parent) in the labor force, and only 4 percent had both parents working full time.

By contrast, in 1988 almost half (49%) had both (or their only) parents in the labor force, and almost one in four (24%) had both parents employed full time. Moreover, it is estimated that, by 1995, nearly two-thirds of all preschoolers will have working mothers (Hofferth and Phillips 1987). Clearly, growing numbers of families are challenged by the need to provide child care.

Who cares for children when their mothers work? Parents choose particular child-care arrangements on the bases of their availability, convenience, reliability, quality, and cost, as well as on the ages and number of their children, their own work schedules, and their personal preferences for one type of care over another.[24] Child care is undeniably a widespread concern among parents of children of all ages, but it presents an especially critical problem when children are young. Most problematic of all is the care of infants.

Infants

Until recently most infants were cared for by their mothers; few mothers with babies under a year old worked outside the home. But this group of women is now the fastest growing segment of the female labor force; by 1990 over half (51.3%) the mothers of infants were employed.

Most infants of working mothers are cared for by relatives, typically the father or the mother's own mother (Floge 1985). But parents use a variety of child-care arrangements, both sequentially, as their children grow older, and concurrently, at different hours of the day or on different days of the week. The best information on trends in child-care arrangements comes from surveys conducted by the U.S. Bureau of the Census (1982, 1983, 1987). These surveys, which focus on the *primary* child-care arrangements used for children of working mothers, document that few infants under one year of age are enrolled in formal day-care centers. However, the proportion grew from 3.6 percent in 1982 to 8.4 percent in 1984–85. By contrast, during the 1984–85 period almost one in five (18%) infants of working mothers were cared for by their fathers and another fifth (20%) were cared for by grandparents.

Preschoolers

Working mothers of preschoolers in the 1980s relied on different child-care arrangements than did working mothers in the 1950s. In May 1958, the Children's Bureau launched the first national survey of the child-care arrangements of employed mothers. It found then that most working mothers of preschoolers fashioned private, informal arrangements in their own homes. Over half (57%) of preschoolers were cared for this way, with only 5 percent in group day care. In fact, almost 90 percent of the children of employed mothers in 1958 were in the care of fathers, siblings, relatives, housekeepers, friends, or neighbors (Select Committee on Children, Youth, and Families 1984).

A National Child-Care Consumer Study conducted in 1975 found that in-home care remained the most popular arrangement in the mid-1970s, although the proportion had shrunk considerably from the 1950s; only 26 percent of preschoolers with employed mothers were cared for in their own homes.

Subsequent studies documented a modest but steady increase in the use of organized child-care arrangements (day-care centers, nursery schools, and preschools)—from 13 percent in 1977 to 16 percent in 1982. By 1984–85, one in four (25%) preschoolers with employed mothers were in day-care or group care centers. Thirty percent of the mothers

Figure 4.3
Trends in Use of Organized Child-Care Facilities for Youngest Child under Age 5 by Employed Mothers, 1958–1985

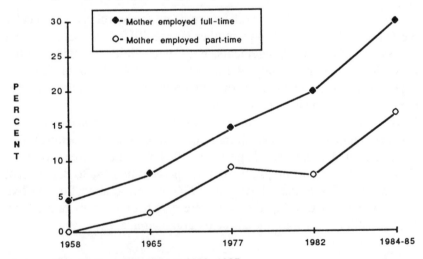

Sources: U.S. Bureau of the Census 1982, 1987.

Note: Data for 1958 and 1965 are for children under age 6.

working full-time used such organized child-care facilities, compared to 17 percent of those employed part-time (see Figure 4.3).[25]

Black mothers were much more likely to use group care (31%) than either white (21%) or Hispanic (21%) mothers. And single-parent mothers were slightly more apt to use organized child care than married women (28% and 24%, respectively). In fact, the greatest increment from 1982 to 1984–85 in the use of organized child-care arrangements occurred among employed wives, increasing by 10 percentage points over that period, and reducing the gap in the use of day-care by wives and single parents.

The reliance on formal child-care arrangements also varies by mothers' education and occupation; about 30 percent of the college-educated mothers and those in managerial or professional occupations placed their preschoolers in day-care or preschool centers in 1984–85. By contrast, only 15 percent of those without a high school education and only 10.5 percent of women in service occupations used such arrangements. These differences may in part reflect the affordability of group care. Studies of low-income women found that child-care costs and the availability of low-cost care (such as a Head Start center) affected these women's employment: the more expensive the child care, the more likely they were to leave the labor force (Blau and Robins, 1989). Additionally, those in lower level occupations, such as service workers, are more likely to work non-day or irregular schedules and have both less access to and less need for day care, given their working hours. As Harriet Presser (1989) notes, the very word *day* care is telling; there is little formal provision for child care at night.

Little change occurred from 1982 to 1984–85 in the proportion (15%) of children under age five cared for in their own homes by their fathers. Fathers were most likely to care for their preschoolers when their wives were employed part-time (reported by 26% of families with the wife working part-time in 1984–85). Single-parent mothers who worked part-time frequently left their children in the care of their grandparents in the children's own home.[26]

Growing maternal employment precipitated an 80 percent increase from 1970 to 1980 in the number of children enrolled in nursery schools—from 1.1 million to 2.0 million. Enrollment in kindergarten, however, remained constant at just over 3.2 million throughout the 1970s. This reflects the fact that preschool, in the form of kindergarten, has virtually become universal for 5-year-olds.

School-Age Children

The principal caretaker of children 5 to 13 years of age is the school, since children in this age group spend most of their daytime hours in the classroom. But, given the time discrepancy between the typical working day and the typical school day, before and after-school care becomes a problem, especially for children whose mothers are employed full-time. Recent estimates of the number of latch-key children—those in elementary school who are not supervised by an adult after school—range widely from 2 to 15 million. Self-care is more likely to be relied on by middle- and upper-income white mothers living in suburban or rural areas (Cain and Hofferth 1989).

However, trends in child care from the 1960s to the 1980s (see Figures 4.4 and 4.5) suggest that only about 12 percent of children aged 6 to 13 whose mothers were employed full-time cared for themselves in 1984, a smaller proportion of latch-key children than in 1965 and 1974. Of the

Figure 4.4
Trends in Care of School-Age Children (6 to 13) of Mothers Employed Full-Time, 1965–1984

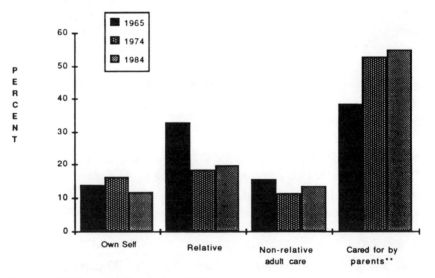

Source: U.S. Bureau of the Census 1987: 5.
Notes: N (thousands): 1965 = 31,315; 1974 = 30,433; 1984 = 26,256.
*Data for 1965 refer to care while mother was working; data for 1974 and 1984 refer to after-school care.

Figure 4.5
Percentage of School-Age Children (5 to 13) with Mothers Employed Full-Time Who Are Not Cared for by an Adult after School, by Age and Race, December 1984

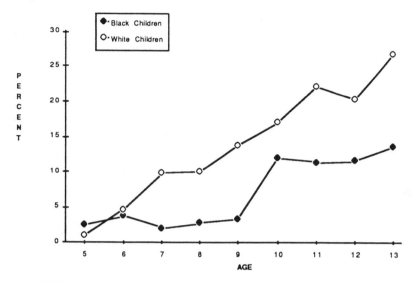

Source: U.S. Bureau of the Census 1987: 12.

28 million children aged 5 to 13 who were enrolled in school in 1984—regardless of their mothers' labor force attachment—only 2 million (7%) spent time after school not in the care of an adult; a half-million (1.9%) were without adult supervision before school; and less than one-third of a million (0.9%) were alone at night. The older of these children are the most likely to be in the latch-key category; about one in five children aged 11–13 had no after-school supervision when the mother worked full-time (see Figure 4.5).

EFFECTS ON CHILDREN'S DEVELOPMENT

I feel that a baby, if I commit myself to a baby, I can't let it go for a week like I can the garden. (Thirty-year-old married woman professional quoted in Gerson 1985:159)

An early and enduring concern—of parents, social scientists, policy-makers, and social commentators—has been the effects on children of having a working mother. Apprehension, which began to blossom in the 1950s, continues to be voiced today. In the 1950s the employment of mothers of young children was seen as a social *problem*; today it is very much a social *fact*. The spotlight in the 1950s focused on negative outcomes; today commentators often point to the positive effects on a child's development. Still, critical questions remain unanswered concerning the long- and short-term consequences of maternal employment for children. Have the actual effects on children changed over the years as more and more women combine mothering with employment? Or is it merely *perceptions* that have changed?

Appraising the effects of maternal employment on children is a formidable task, and investigators have arrived at no single—or simple— answer. On the positive side, research portrays working mothers as role models who enhance the aspirations and self-concepts of their daughters and promote more egalitarian sex-role attitudes in both sons and daughters. Scholars also see as beneficial the enhanced participation of fathers in child rearing and the independence training working parents provide to their children. On the other hand, they cite problems such as less adequate supervision, maternal guilt (and, hence, overcompensation), emotional stress, and even maternal "deprivation" as constituting the negative side of the ledger. [27]

Unfortunately, research on this topic over the last three decades is more notable for its deficiencies than for its confident conclusions. Studies typically divide mothers into one of two groups, working and not working, ignoring whether they work full-time or part-time, whether they want to work, and whether they have been employed for a week, a year, or "forever." Moreover, any links found between maternal employment and children's attitudes or behavior are often merely described, not accompanied by explanations as to why or how such relationships came about.

Missing in this body of research is an appreciation of the changing demography of family life. More children have working mothers than ever before, but the children of employed mothers are more likely than those with homemaker mothers to be the only child or to have only one brother or sister, to have older parents, and to be in families with higher levels of income. These children are also more likely than others to spend some portion of their childhood in a single-parent family. Researchers seeking to determine the consequences of having a working mother must take this changing family context into account. Moreover, the effects of maternal employment depend upon the child's own personality and temperament (as well as gender), the family's resources and stage in the life course, the kinds of child-care arrangements made, parental attitudes and values, and the parents' working conditions—as well as the age of the child.

Infants and Preschoolers

Particularly troubling to those who extol mother care are the possible harmful effects of maternal employment on the development of very young children. However, the most reliable social science evidence produced to date suggests few such injurious effects.

Evaluating outcomes for infants and preschoolers requires the right yardsticks. What measures can be used to gauge the costs—if any—to babies of having their mothers in the labor force? Researchers typically concentrate on children's cognitive and emotional development (aspirations, self-concept, and so on) and their social adjustment. For young infants, a commonly used criterion has been their attachment to their mothers, as evidenced by their response to strangers and strange situations.

Ellen Hock (1980, 1978) accomplished some of the best early work on this subject. In her longitudinal studies of the first year of infants' lives, she found that the employment of the mother was not related to the quality of the mother-child relationship, the infant's developmental level, or the type of care giving provided by the mother. Indeed, Hock discovered that the infants of employed mothers were more accepting of contacts with strangers. What mattered most, in Hock's studies, was the congruency between the mother's attitude about maternal care and her actual labor force status. This brings to mind the distinctions made in Chapter 3 among captive, conflicted, copers, and committed women workers. Hock found that women whose status was inconsistent with their beliefs about proper care had infants who were more likely to exhibit "negative maternal reunion behavior"; in other words, they were more apt to avoid reunion with their mothers when exposed to a "strange situation" (see also Schwartz 1983).

In examining the experiences of both black and white middle-class children, Hock found no difference. A study conducted by F. F. Cherry and E. L. Eaton (1977) of lower income black families also found no differences in the physical or cognitive development of the children (aged 1 to 7) related to the employment of their mothers.

Other, more recent, investigations of mother-infant attachment have reported no statistically significant differences in attachment between the infants of working and nonworking mothers. However, two studies did find a larger proportion of "insecure" infants among those whose mothers were employed. And two other studies reported a higher proportion of insecure attachments by sons in families with employed mothers.

These gender differences are intriguing. Urie Bronfenbrenner and his colleagues found that mothers employed full-time were the least likely to portray their sons positively and most likely to describe their daughters positively. Moreover, in the most detailed analysis to date, using data from a 1986 survey of 4-year-olds, maternal employment was judged to have a negative effect on the cognitive development of boys in higher income families (Desai, Chase-Lansdale and Michael 1989).[28]

The employment of mothers may produce differences in the behavior of both parents. One study found that working couples were less likely to engage in quiet play or discussions with their preschoolers than were traditional single-earner couples. Moreover, in two-earner families, there may be less, rather than more, interaction between infants and their fathers. Mothers employed outside the home for much of the day may dote exclusively on their infants after work, leaving little time for fathers to spend with their babies. One study of three-month-old infants found that fathers with working wives were less likely to hold, touch, and play with their babies than were those with homemaker wives (Zaslow et al. 1985, 1989).

Related research on the effects of day care has led to similarly ambiguous conclusions.[29] But the most recent studies on this hotly contested issue have used more complex research designs to clarify the many uncertainties that surround it. For example, several studies examine the history of child-care arrangements *throughout* the child's preschool years, rather than simply looking at the situation at a single point in time. One such study examined the combined effects of different child-care arrangements and family influences on preschoolers' levels of compliance, finding that boys seemed somewhat adversely affected by poor-quality child care (Howes and Olenick 1986). In following eighty-six preschoolers over three years, Howes (1988) found that high-quality, stable child care during the preschool years was predictive of adjustment and academic achievement in the first grade. Maternal employment was less important than were the parents' education and the nature of the child care. As Howes points out, factors such as maternal employment and day care must be "unpackaged in order to understand family and child-care influences on children's development" (1988:56; see also Phillips, McCartney, and Scarr 1987; Clarke-Stewart 1989).

In another study, third graders were examined to determine the effects of various child-care histories during the preschool years, controlling for gender, social class, and current after-school care (Vandell and Corasaniti 1988, 1990). The researchers found that children who began full-time child care during infancy were less compliant and had less satisfactory peer relationships, lower grades, and poorer work habits than those who began such care later in life. Full-time care was associated with more negative outcomes than either part-time or exclusive maternal care. These results suggest that extensive child care during infancy may have negative developmental outcomes. However, the study gives no consideration of the quality of the care or of any family factors that might contribute to these effects.

Recent reviews of research in this area by psychologist Jay Belksy led him to caution that substitute care during the child's first year may have long-term negative consequences, leading to "subsequent aggression, noncompliance and possibly even social withdrawal in the preschool and early school years" (1987a:7). The very tentativeness of Belsky's conclusions is, however, sustained by many of his colleagues, who feel that either (1) maternal employment has no direct child outcomes but operates through other factors in the family environment (Gottfried and Gottfried 1988) or (2) no definitive conclusions can be drawn from the data at hand (Bronfenbrenner 1991).[30]

Middle Childhood

When children reach school age, their school performance becomes a readily available and more easily interpretable outcome. A series of studies of Canadian children conducted in the 1970s by D. Gold and D. Andres found a negative relationship between maternal employment and academic performance for working-class boys, as measured by language and mathematics tests.[31] But an earlier study of black children (Woods 1972) found full-time maternal employment to have *positive* consequences for school-aged children, with children of employed mothers scoring higher on social adjustment and intelligence measures. But the best scores were achieved by children whose mothers enjoyed their work (i.e., the committed), once again pointing to the importance of the mother's own orientation toward work. On the other hand, Woods found that, in families with working mothers, girls were less supervised than boys and that with less supervision they also exhibited poorer cognitive development.

In 1986, significant numbers of employed parents in a nationwide survey reported that their work had a positive effect on their children's school-related activities. Many felt that it improved their child's performance in school (41%), increased attendance at school (45%) and promptness in arriving at school (47%), enhanced conduct and deportment in school (46%), and facilitated participation in extracurricular activities. Similar positive outcomes were also seen as resulting from the spouse's job. These beneficial outcomes were most often mentioned by parents in white-collar jobs, especially those in professional and managerial jobs.[32]

Still, these opinions, expressed by a cross-section of American parents, do not capture the *actual experiences* of children. As Martha Moorehouse (1991) points out, the processes by which maternal employment translates into fewer (or more) shared activities at home may be the key in understanding the mechanisms linking maternal employment to child outcomes. The fact is that the impacts of maternal employment on children's school behavior and performance remain both controversial and difficult to ascertain.[33]

Adolescence and Early Adulthood

Another issue of common concern is the effect of maternal employment on the gender-role orientations and career aspirations of children, adolescents, and young adults. Most research on these links focuses on daughters, assuming that they, more than sons, should be influenced by having a working mother as a role model. But the relationship of maternal employment to the attitudes, aspirations, and eventual achievements of the daughter is confounded by considerations of the timing of the mother's employment during the daughter's childhood, possible cohort variations (i.e., differences between being a child in the 1950s and in the 1980s), and such other factors as the mother's educational and occupational level. Because studies seldom take these contingencies into account, their findings regarding a mother's influence on her daughter are inconsistent and even contradictory. Some conclude that the daughters of working mothers have more favorable attitudes toward employment, greater self-assurance, and independence and are more likely to move into typically male occupations. Others report weak or no relationships between maternal employment and sex-role attitudes, career salience, or aspirations. Similarly, research findings regarding the effects on the daughters' eventual occupational attainments are also contradictory. Moreover, whatever salutary effects the mother's occupational status may have on her daughter's own attainment may well be limited to the daughter's first job. The achievements of older adult women could well be influenced more by their own circumstances (educational level, age and number of children, work experience, and so on) than by their mothers' experiences and achievements.[34]

It may be that the very real impediments to combining work and family affect the aspirations and expectations of young women even more than the particular experiences of their own mothers. Consider, for example, the research finding that high school girls with high occupational goals plan to marry late and have few children, perhaps because they recognize the incompatibilities of family and career roles (cf. Waite and Stolzenberg 1976).

Trends and Contexts

Do children today have a greater or a lower sense of self-worth, autonomy, and independence as a consequence of their mothers' employment? Are differences between boys and girls in their attitudes and behavior diminishing? Do young women today have higher levels of educational and occupational aspiration than earlier generations? To answer such questions we cannot simply treat maternal employment as what Bronfenbrenner calls a "social address" (1982:7), a label pinned to children without examining its timing in the child's (and mother's) life, its duration, and its context. So too must we consider the meaning of employment for the mother, the father, and the total family unit. All of these factors influence the child's environment, including the processes that go on between care givers and the child and, hence, the child's development (see Figure 4.6).

The *fact* of maternal employment alone has little meaning with regard to children's development. What matters is its *context*—the circumstances surrounding a mother's employment—the factors that may render it more or less salutary or problematic for the development of children, and its impact on *process*—how employment affects ongoing behavior and relationships. For example, a study of white working-class families with at least one school-aged child in the home found that boys whose mothers were exposed to stressful conditions on the job were less likely to report positive maternal involvement and supportiveness (Piotrkowski and Katz 1982). This outcome, in turn, was related to reports by the boys of more symptoms of depression, lower self-esteem, and less feeling of competence in relations with peers. Also, the mother's hours on the job were positively linked to her son's self-esteem and feelings of competence with peers and with a better father-son relationship. However, neither the benefits nor the liabilities of a mother's employment reported for boys was found for girls, suggesting that there may be significant gender

Figure 4.6
Linking Trends in Maternal Employment to Children's Development

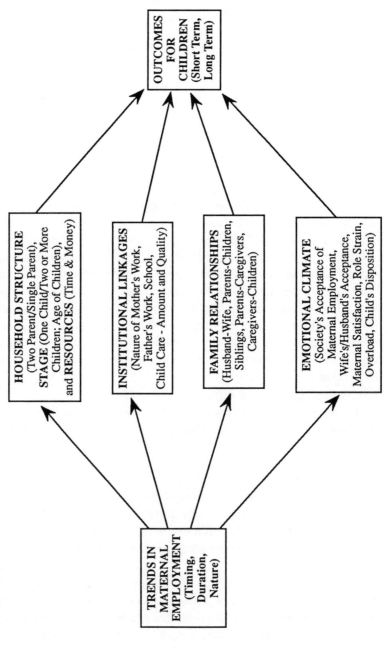

differences in the mental health outcomes of parental job conditions. This study, like the others discussed earlier reporting gender differences, underscores the complexity of the "working mother" issue. And there are no studies of maternal employment that adequately capture the processes that go on between care givers and the child—what actually happens in the child's daily life.

Maternal employment is by now commonplace, with previous distinctions by marital status and race substantially narrowing. Preschoolers and school-aged children are increasingly apt to have a working mother regardless of whether she is married or single, black or white. And even young infants are more likely to have a working than a stay-at-home mother. Still, as developmental psychologist Sandra Scarr (1984) concludes, as a society we have not untangled the costs and benefits of this remarkable social change. This uncertainty, she notes, reflects conflicting cultural values more than conclusive social science findings.

As we have seen, to date research has produced no simple, straightforward findings regarding the effects on children of having a working mother. But we can draw the following tentative conclusions: (1) daughters appear to benefit from having an employed mother more than do sons; (2) the effects of maternal employment on sons is ambiguous, with possibly negative effects in middle-class families; (3) maternal employment affects not only the mother-child relationship but also the father-child relationship; (4) the mother's attitude toward her employment (or nonemployment) may be more important than the employment itself; (5) characteristics of the mother's job (such as part-time versus full-time) are essential in examining child outcomes; and (6) young children when exposed to group situations get sick more often than those cared for in individual homes (Johansen, Leibowitz, and Waite 1988).

Actual research findings on the effects on children of having a working mother fall well short of portraying trends over time. My judgment is that the processes that go on in a child's immediate environment may well have changed from the 1950s to the 1990s, regardless of whether the mother is employed. Social observers lamenting the "bureaucratization" of childhood are correct in proclaiming that decreasing numbers of young children are being cared for in their own homes (cf. Elkind 1981; Postman 1982). Not only are fewer mothers now full-time homemakers, those who are in the labor force are more likely today than in the past to arrange for child care outside of their homes (see Figure 4.7).

Not only the location of care giving, but also the day-to-day interactions between the care givers and the children have changed. What counts is the quality of care, whether in or out of the home, whether by a mother,

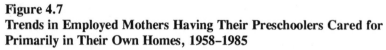

Figure 4.7
Trends in Employed Mothers Having Their Preschoolers Cared for
Primarily in Their Own Homes, 1958–1985

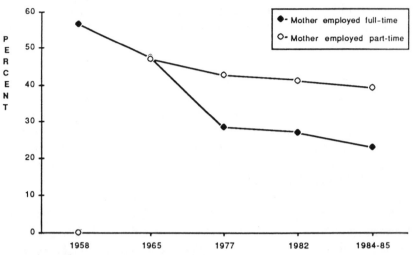

Sources: U.S. Bureau of the Census 1982, 1987.

father, or day-care provider (see Clarke-Stewart 1989; Hoffman 1989; Bronfenbrenner 1991). But full-time homemakers are increasingly iso-lated in their care-giving role, since relatives, friends, and neighbors are themselves working. With fewer women as full-time homemakers there is less support from the community for that role, and the rewards are not the same as those provided in times when most mothers were at home caring for their children. Having a stay-at-home mother may or may not represent quality care, depending on the supports available in the neighborhood and community as well as within the family, the mother's own preferences, and her attitudes toward mothering.

On the other hand, employed mothers must increasingly resort to a patchwork arrangement of care. Some may well be of a higher quality than others. This is certainly true of day-care arrangements. Child-care providers, among the poorest paid of all workers, often are minimally trained and are prone to frequent turnover, both of which affect the quality of care.

We know that the key to optimal human development is a stable, predictable environment and that in hectic, unpredictable situations the processes linking children to their care givers begin to deteriorate (Bronfenbrenner 1991). Yet the current reality of American society is that the daily life of the child is frequently disjointed, neither stable nor predictable.

From a child development perspective, the important issue regarding employment and child-care arrangements is whether they make family life easier to conduct. For many families the mother's salary is essential for the family economy, and her employment is beneficial to her own emotional well-being. At the same time, maternal employment in the context of today's institutional constraints makes family life both more unpredictable and more hectic. We provide no systematic supports for families in the United States, regardless of whether the mother is working; therefore, American families with young children are increasingly placed at risk.

It is unquestionably true that, in tandem with the growth of maternal employment and the rising isolation of the nuclear family, raising children has become increasingly problematic. Because child care has been seen as the exclusive province of women, this has been defined as a woman's issue, not a man's, and certainly not a societal issue. And it is women's, not men's, employment that is seen as the culprit. But we are living a transition in progress and, given the shifts that have occurred in societal expectations for men and women, there is no accepted definition of what constitutes "proper" parenting for either mothers or fathers. To be sure, mothering today, as in the past, still involves arranging family activities within the schedule constraints imposed by outside institutions—the father's workplace, schools, health care and other service providers, and retail stores. What is different is that additional timetables—those of the mother's workplace and the day-care providers—must now be taken into account, with an ever-dwindling number of "discretionary" hours in the day.

NOTES

1. Data are taken from the General Social Survey (Mason and Lu 1988).

2. There is a range of studies and reviews on this topic (Berk and Berk 1979; Berk 1985; Blood and Wolfe 1960; Geerken and Gove 1983; Farkas 1976; Robinson 1977; Pleck 1983, 1985; Walker and Woods 1976; Huber and Spitze 1983; Coverman 1985; Hill and Stafford 1974, 1980; Juster 1985; Coverman and Sheley 1986; Hochschild 1989; Menaghan and Parcel 1990).

3. Although some early community studies reported that husbands of employed wives were more likely to share *somewhat* in household tasks (Hoffman 1963b; Blood and Wolfe 1960) than men married to full-time homemakers, nationally representative time-use studies showed no difference by wife's employment status. However, studies did report that changes had

occurred by the late 1970s (Coverman 1985; Huber and Spitze 1983; Nickols and Metzen 1982; Weingarten 1978; Pleck 1985).

4. For overviews of this shift, see Gecas (1976), Ericksen, Yancey, and Ericksen (1979), Berk and Berk (1979), Nock and Kingston (1988), Pleck (1985), Coverman and Sheley (1986), Robinson (1985), and Juster (1985).

5. For the effects of husband's income and wife's earnings, see Ericksen, Yancey, and Ericksen (1979), and Ross, Mirowsky, and Huber (1983). For the effects of the presence of children, see Berk and Berk (1979), Berk (1985), Juster (1985), Coverman (1985), and Coverman and Sheley (1986). For education effects, see Ericksen, Yancey, and Ericksen (1979), Walker and Woods (1976), Duncan and Duncan (1978), and Ross, Mirowsky, and Huber (1983). For the effect of the husband's work hours, see Crouter et al. (1987), Pleck (1983, 1985), Robinson (1977), and Walker and Woods (1976).

6. Shifts by cohort are reported in Farkas (1976) and Pleck (1985). Changes by race are seen by contrasting the studies conducted by Farkas (1976) and Ericksen, Yancey, and Ericksen (1979) with those conducted by Ross, Mirowsky, and Huber (1983) and Coverman and Sheley (1986). The overall trends in men's involvement in housework and child care by no means illustrate a steady linear increase over the years. Comparisons of surveys conducted in Detroit in 1955 and 1971 reveal no systematic movement over that period toward equality in the distribution of household tasks (Duncan and Duncan 1978). A time-use study of 750 urban households conducted in the 1970s found only a minimal increase in the husbands' involvement accompanying wives' employment (Berk and Berk 1979; see also general overviews by Miller and Garrison 1982; Pleck 1985).

Part of the difficulty in gauging long-term trends in the sexual division of labor is the fact that social scientists use quite different measures of it, ranging from single-item questions to complicated time diaries. Adding to the complexity of interpretation, husbands and wives at all stages of the life course are typically grouped together in a single analysis.

7. See, for example, Daniels and Weingarten (1982), Coverman and Sheley (1986), Juster (1985), and Pleck (1985).

8. Prior to 1910 the traditional middle-class arrangement was for a servant to do the housework. Even during World War II wives typically joined the labor force only when their husbands were drafted. Even women without children felt a responsibility to take care of their husbands (Long 1958:125).

9. Pleck (1986); Pleck, Lamb, and Levine (1985); Lamb and Sagi (1983). For the feminist theoretical perspective, see also Hartmann (1976), Sokoloff (1980, 1988), and Walby (1986).

10. For an exchange perspective, see Bernard (1981) and Scanzoni (1970, 1978). Several early studies (Blood 1963; Hoffman 1963b; Bahr 1974; Gillespie 1971) and reviews (Moore and Hofferth 1979; Rallings and Nye 1979) are available.

11. See Bott (1957), Blood (1963), Dizard (1968), Aldous (1983), and Simpson and England (1981).

12. This perspective also has a long tradition of acceptance in the sociological literature (Parsons 1942; Parsons and Bales 1966), and it is embraced by economist Gary Becker (1981) as well.

13. There is both early (Axelson 1963; Nye 1963) and more recent evidence (Staines and Pleck 1983; Pleck 1985; Hochschild 1989).

14. See the discussions by Parsons (1942) and by Oppenheimer (1977). A study by Philliber and Hiller (1983), for example, reports that, when the wife's job is more prestigious than her husband's, either she is likely to move to a lower status job or the marriage is apt to end in divorce. Other investigators do not confirm this finding (Oppenheimer 1977; Huber and Spitze 1980).

15. Some studies report no differences (Campbell, Converse, and Rodgers 1976; Wright 1978; Locksley 1980; Glenn and Weaver 1978); others have found that husbands of employed wives were less satisfied with their marriages than single-earner husbands (Geerken and Gove 1983; Crouter et al. 1987).

16. Three other studies, also with small or select samples, have produced inconsistent results regarding the psychological well-being of husbands of employed wives (Burke and Weir 1976; Booth 1977, 1979; Roberts and O'Keefe 1981). Campbell (1984) notes that, during World War II, women in unhappy marriages, on the verge of divorce, prepared for this contingency by getting a job. Hence, any correlation between the wife's employment and the husband's dissatisfaction is not surprising. For the salutary consequences of fathers' child care, see also Baruch and Barnett (1986a).

17. See Moen (1989) and Wethington (1992).

18. The age of children is more important than their number in establishing the amount of time spent in child care—at least for mothers (Berk 1985; Pleck 1985; Coverman and Sheley 1986).

19. Studies conducted over the 1970s document this fact (Vanek 1974, 1980; Walker and Woods 1976; Robinson 1977; Geerken and Gove 1983).

20. See Sanik and Mauldin (1986) for women giving up sleep and Hochschild (1989) for examples of women's double day. Similarly, working wives during World War II also cut back on their hours of sleep to cope with their multiple demands (Campbell 1984).

21. See Opinion Research Corporation (1987). However, "economic necessity" is a social decision. If the employment of wives and mothers is not socially sanctioned, as was the case in the United States prior to World War II, then expected standards of living will adjust accordingly. And, as more women are employed, the definition of what is an adequate or comfortable standard of living changes (Hernandez 1989). The wife's employment is also a protection against the ravages of unemployment (Moen, Kain, and Elder 1983).

22. See Opinion Research Corporation (1987:39). Some studies look at morale (Birnbaum 1975; Ferree 1976, 1987; Veroff, Douvan, and Kulka 1981; Kessler and McRae 1982); others look at preference for employment (Gove and Zeiss 1987; Whitham and Moen 1992).

23. See Nock and Kingston (1988), Hood and Golden (1979), Presser (1986, 1988, 1989), Presser and Cain (1983), and Staines and Pleck (1984).

24. The answer cannot be definitive because studies of child-care arrange-ments use different samples and ask different questions (Dickenson 1975; Duncan and Hill 1975, 1977; Hofferth 1979; Hofferth and Phillips 1987; Shortlidge, Suter, and Waite 1977; Westinghouse 1971; Low and Spindler 1968). Moreover, Leibowitz and colleagues suggest that the most appropriate care may vary by age of the child (cf. Cain and Hofferth 1989; Kamerman and Kahn 1979; Floge 1985, 1989; Kamerman 1983).

25. See U.S. Bureau of the Census (1975a, 1983, 1987). The data are for preschoolers under age 5. Recall that we have data on *employed* mothers only.

26. Twenty-six percent of single parents used grandparents as caretakers in the 1984–85 survey (U.S. Bureau of the Census 1987).

27. See reviews by Hoffman (1961, 1963a, 1979, 1984, 1987, 1989), Nye and Hoffman (1963), Hoffman and Nye (1974), Bronfenbrenner and Crouter (1982), and Belsky and Rovine (1988).

28. No differences were found by Easterbrooks and Goldberg (1988), Hoffman (1984), or Owen and Cox (1988). More insecure infants, among those whose mothers were employed, were found by Barglow, Vaughn, and Molitor (1987). Insecure attachments by sons were reported by Chase-Lans-dale and Owen (1987) and Belksy and Rovine (1988). Parents' perceptions are discussed in Bronfenbrenner, Alvarez, and Henderson (1984) and Bronfenbrenner and Crouter (1982). The most sophisticated study to date was accomplished by Desai, Chase-Lansdale, and Michael (1989). This study was based on a survey of 4-year-old children of women originally surveyed in the National Longitudinal Survey. Cognitive development was measured with a widely used, standardized scale (Peabody Picture Vocabulary Test). In this study, a variety of demographic, economic, and social background factors were controlled in the analysis, lending greater credence to the findings.

29. See reviews by Clarke-Stewart (1977, 1989), Crouter, Belsky, and Spanier (1984), Belsky and Steinberg (1978), Belsky, Lerner, and Spanier (1984), Belsky (1987a, 1987b), Belsky and Rovine (1988), and Vandell and Corasaniti (1988, 1990). In 1984 a developmental psychologist, Jay Belsky, and his colleagues concluded that the preponderance of the evidence—albeit mostly on children from white, middle-class families—suggested that day care has "neither beneficial nor adverse effects on the intellectual development (as measured by standardized tests) of most children" and "little influence on the child's emotional ties to his or her mother [other than *transient* distress]" (Belsky, Lerner, and Spanier 1984:202–4). However, Belsky, apparently troubled by more recent studies, reexamined the evidence to date and con-cluded that "extensive nonparental care initiated in the first year . . . is a risk factor in the development of insecure infant-parent attachment" (1987a:7). His assessment of the potentially negative effects of nonparental care has generated considerable controversy among developmental psychologists. One issue of contention is the interpretation of the data at hand. A second is the validity of the "strange situation" measure as an index of attachment because children of

employed mothers are accustomed to encounters with strangers (Vaughn, Deane, and Waters 1985).

30. See Belsky (1986, 1987a, b) and Belsky and Rovine (1988), as well as available reviews (Bronfenbrenner and Crouter 1982; Kamerman and Hayes 1982; Clarke-Stewart 1989; Hoffman 1989; Scarr, Phillips, and McCartney 1989).

31. See Gold and Andres (1978a, 1978b) and Gold, Andres, and Glorieux (1979). See also Banducci (1967).

32. But note that these are the self-reports of parents and are not based on objective evidence, such as school records.

33. See discussions by Heyns (1982), Heyns and Catsambis (1986), Spitze (1988), and Hoffman (1989).

34. Favorable attitudes are seen in Almquist and Angrist (1971). Greater self-assurance is documented in Hoffman (1972) and nontraditional occupations in Tangri (1972). Weak or no relationships are reported in Bielby (1978), and Thornton, Alwin, and Camburn (1983). In terms of occupational attainment, no effect was reported by Bielby (1978), and positive effects were reported by Rosenfeld (1978) and Marini (1980). For effects on adult achievement, see Marini (1980) and the general discussions in Miller and Garrison (1982) and Baruch (1972).

5 IMPLICATIONS FOR EMPLOYERS, UNIONS, AND GOVERNMENTS

> Our current public policies are anachronistic. They assume a traditional worker and family which no longer exist.
> *(Spalter-Roth and Hartmann 1991)*

Henry Ford reportedly said that "the future ain't what it used to be." As we saw in the last chapter, nothing could be more true about the American family. The employment of wives and mothers, especially mothers of young children, in tandem with the other trends discussed in Chapter 2, has significantly altered the shape and character of families over the last fifty years. But the world of work also has undergone extraordinary transformations during the last five decades. Changes in the structure of the economy and the composition of the work force have had broad repercussions on individuals, families, and society.

THE CHANGING COMPOSITION OF THE LABOR FORCE

In less than a generation, the nation's pattern of employment has been radically altered, from one in which most married women stayed home, to one in which nearly everyone is paid to work. Because so much of the change has occurred since 1960, the society has not fully digested its implications. (Johnston and Packer 1987:87)

A particularly pervasive, long-term economic change has been the growth of the service sector, with the shift of employment from manufacturing industries (e.g., steel, auto, and textile) to service industries (e.g., communications, public utilities, trade, finance, and government). This move to a service-based economy has produced a strong demand for women workers. Given the limited supply of available single women in relation to the high demand for new workers, wives—including those with children—have been attracted into the labor force.[1]

The forces shaping the American economy suggest that the demand for women workers will continue unabated. The Bureau of Labor Statistics predicts that 90 percent of the 16 million new jobs created from 1987 through 1995 will be in service industries. That, coupled with expected labor force shortages, undoubtedly will draw even more mothers of young children into paid employment.

Part-Time and Temporary Work

Concomitant with the shift to a service economy has been the growth of part-time and temporary jobs. Service industries seldom require the scheduling rigidities endemic to assembly-line work or continuous production, making service jobs more amenable to part-time or short-term employment. In 1955 only about one in ten U.S. workers was putting in fewer than thirty-five hours a week; by 1988 about one in six was working part-time. In fact, in the 1980s the part-time work force grew about twice as fast as total employment in the U.S. economy, increasing from 16.3 million workers in 1980 to 19.8 million in 1988. The growth of temporary jobs is even more striking, moving from a minuscule 0.4 million in 1980 to 1.1 million in 1988, a 175 percent increase (Belous 1989; Nine to Five 1986).

Not surprisingly, given their child-care and other domestic responsibilities, women hold the majority of part-time and temporary jobs. In 1985 over two-thirds (67.6%) of the part-timers were women, as were almost two-thirds (64.2%) of the temporary workers. But the proliferation of these jobs is far more a result of the changing economy than a response to the needs of women balancing work and family roles. Employers recruit such a "contingent work force" because it is flexible and encumbers significantly lower labor costs. Still, these working arrangements do offer women more flexibility and discretionary time in reconciling their work and family obligations. But they also exact a heavy price: Part-time and temporary jobs tend to be low-wage jobs with few benefits, typically without security and providing little opportunity for advancement.[2]

for forty years. However, the gap in wages between men and women is beginning to narrow (Blau and Ferber 1986).

The proliferation of wives and mothers of young children in the work force has, in fact, led to still more "female" jobs. Their very labor force participation has created the need for additional service jobs—child-care, restaurant, and laundry workers—as well the need for more sales clerks and cashiers to expand the hours retail businesses remain open (Norwood 1985). Increasingly, what was once women's unpaid work at home has become paid work—still for women—in the service economy.

Trends

In 1940, on the eve of World War II, only one in four (25%) workers was female. By 1945 women had become 29 percent of the labor force, falling slightly (to 27%) in 1947 following the war, but climbing back to 29 percent by 1950 (see Figure 5.1). Since 1950 the trend has been continuously upward. Women have accounted for 60 percent of the increase in the labor force over the last four decades, and in 1990 they represented 45 percent of the work force. Moreover, two-thirds of the new entrants into the labor force between now and the year 2000 are

Figure 5.1
Trends in Women as a Percent of the Labor Force, Annual Averages

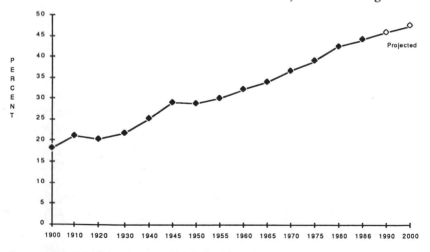

Sources: Bureau of the Census 1975; Johnston 1987: 85.

Note: 1940–1945 data refer to persons 14 years and over.

Men's Jobs, Women's Jobs

The expanding service sector has drawn women into the lab(
but they remain, for the most part, in sex-segregated occι
Throughout the 1970s and 1980s there was very little chang
proportions of women in traditionally "female" jobs, such as clei
household workers. What did change was the number of women
into traditionally male occupations (Reskin and Hartmann 1986
1989; Reskin 1984, 1988).

While women are disproportionately the secretaries, wai
nurses, and elementary schoolteachers of American society, stil
are moving into "men's" jobs. In 1950 only 14 percent of the
executives, administrators, and managers were women; by 1ς
proportion had more than tripled to 40 percent. In 1950 a minusc
percent of all engineers were women; by 1989 that had reach
percent. In 1950 only 4.1 percent of lawyers and judges were v
by 1989 this had more than quadrupled to 19 percent (see Jacobş
Reskin and Roos 1990).

As women began to move into traditional male occupations, the
and 1980s saw a modest decline in occupational sex segregation occ
at all age levels. This suggests a broad pattern of change rather thar
only for the youngest cohorts of women. Women of all ages enter
reentering the labor force are increasingly likely to move into male
inated occupations (Jacobs 1989; Reskin and Roos 1990). Racial (
ences in occupational segregation are also declining (Farley 1984)

Still, despite these sometimes dramatic and unquestionably impe
strides, most women remain in traditionally female jobs. For exai
98 percent of all secretaries in 1970 were female; ten years latei
proportion female was 99 percent. By 1989 women still accounte
95 percent of all secretaries, stenographers, and typists. What is
striking is the relative stability of occupational segregation by gei
Despite the women's movement, economic trends, changing pι
opinion, and equal opportunity legislation, women continue to clustι
a restricted range of occupations.[3]

Social scientists maintain that the reasons women remain concentrι
in these low-paying "female" occupations include discrimination (des
its legal prohibition), the perpetuation of traditional gender norms,
women's own assessment as to the kinds of jobs they can mesh with tl
changing family responsibilities.[4] The costs to women of this persis
occupational segregation are most clearly revealed by the average wa
they earn relative to men, which has remained below the 70 percent le

expected to be women. By the twenty-first century, labor force experts predict that almost half (48%) of all workers will be female, a sizable portion of whom will be women with young children (Johnston and Packer 1987).

Labor force authorities also predict that in response to technological change, population trends, and international competition: (1) there is likely to be a labor force shortage within the next fifteen years as the pool of young workers continues to diminish and the trend toward early retirement continues unabated; (2) the skill requirements of the labor force will rise; and (3) workers may have to change jobs five or six times during their work lives. The emerging shortage of workers is already increasing the demand for women in the work force (Johnston and Packer 1987). The number of Hispanic women in the work force is expected to increase markedly from 3.1 million to 5.8 million, an 85 percent increase. Black women workers are expected to increase by one-third.

But place this new labor force demography in context. What has changed is the ratio of working women to working men. What has changed is the ratio of husbands with working wives to husbands who are sole breadwinners. What has changed is the proportion of women who are employed single parents. What has changed is the proportion of workers coping with child-care responsibilities. What have *not* changed in any major way are the basic structures and conditions of employment. Work place policies, patterns, and practices remain largely geared to a traditional family with a father as the breadwinner and a mother as the homemaker.

THE FAMILY AS A WORK PLACE ISSUE

The cost of employing women in management is greater than the cost of employing men. This is a jarring statement partly because it is true but mostly because it is something people are reluctant to talk about. (Schwartz 1989:65)

The above statement, which introduced an article by Felice Schwartz (president and founder of Catalyst, a nonprofit organization promoting the career development of women), set off a storm of controversy. Should women who plan to have children be relegated to some secondary "mommy track" given that their family responsibilities inevitably encroach upon their work careers? It is true that the progressive "feminization" of the work force has caused family considerations increasingly to intrude into the job and vice versa. At least 90 percent of the women entering the labor force are expected to become pregnant during the course of their work lives. Sandra Hofferth and Deborah Phillips (1987) predict that by 1995 two-thirds of all preschoolers will have employed mothers. As Schwartz points out, the fact that women have babies can be a "costly distraction" (Gallese 1989:33). However, this cannot be dismissed as merely a women's issue. Most men, too, become fathers, and about 60 percent of employed men have wives who are also working (see Figure 5.2). Growing numbers of men as well as women must coordinate their jobs with their spouses' jobs and with several forms of child care.

Employers as well as government officials and social observers are beginning to voice concern about the impacts of family exigencies on worker availability, stability, commitment, and performance.[5]

Worker Availability and Stability

Whenever possible, women choose jobs and working hours that will mesh with their child-care responsibilities and with the demands and constraints (especially geographical) of their husbands' jobs.[6] Difficulties in arranging time off for childbirth and child care mean that some women who leave the labor force would rather be working. For example, a 1982

Figure 5.2
Trends in Husband-Wife Dual-Earner and Traditional Single-Earner Families, 1968–1986

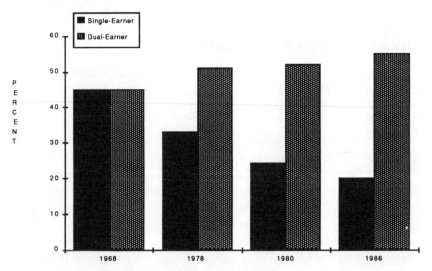

Sources: Hayghe 1981; Bureau of Labor Statistics 1986.

survey of nonemployed mothers of preschoolers found that over one-fourth (26%) reported that they would be looking for work if day care were available (U.S. Bureau of the Census 1983). A study of low-income mothers in the 1970s found they were more likely to stop working when child care was less accessible or less affordable (Blau and Robins 1989).

Many employers view women workers as less dependable, given to higher turnover and absenteeism than men. In part, the image of the reliable male worker exists precisely because women have taken up the slack at home. Men who are husbands and fathers have been able to concentrate their time and energy on their jobs only because someone else (a wife) is overseeing the household. Even though they themselves may be working, wives and mothers continue to administer child-care arrangements as well as minister to their children's needs. Dana Friedman of the Families and Work Institute suggests that men's lower absentee rates are possible because they assume fewer child-care responsibilities. Absenteeism is not, in her words, a "woman's problem" but a "family solution" (1986a:28).

As part of this "family solution," women persist in choosing jobs that maximize their flexibility and frequently either leave the labor force or move to part-time work when family demands escalate —as when a baby is born.[7] Workers and employers alike acknowledge that women use their personal sick leave or vacation time to care for sick children or to fill in when child care is disrupted.[8] Consequently, it is not surprising that women are absent from work more frequently than their male counterparts.

Work Commitment and Productivity

If a woman is married she may be seen as lacking commitment to the labor force; if she is not married (or is married and does not have children) she may be seen as unstable because she *will* get married or *will have* children. (Rosenfeld 1980:588)

Employers often view women—regardless of their marital status or family obligations—as less psychologically invested in their jobs than men (Nollen 1982). In point of fact, however, research findings show that women typically report high levels of psychological commitment to their work (Bielby and Bielby 1984, 1989). Moen and Smith (1986) found, surprisingly, that the most committed among women workers are part-timers, who may be using part-time jobs as a strategy for remaining in the work force when family obligations are the most demanding.

The impact of family responsibilities on worker productivity is difficult to measure. For the most part there is only anecdotal evidence, such as what has come to be known as the "three o'clock syndrome," referring to the reduced productivity and higher accident rates that occur as employees begin to think about their children returning home from school.[9] Just as employers (and researchers) find it difficult to measure productivity satisfactorily, so too do they find it hard to measure potential spillovers from family to work. Still, there is growing agreement that having mothers of young children on the job is bound to affect worker behavior.

Many employers suggest that policies supportive of working parents can be justified only if it is clear that these supports will enhance productivity. Should future studies produce unambiguous findings about the costs to *employers* of work/family dilemmas this would doubtlessly encourage them to adopt employment policies more supportive of the workers who are also parents. But, as Kamerman and Kahn note, the productivity criterion is not equally applied to other practices: "Corporations, for example, do not use productivity as the measure of whether or not they support executive training, they simply do it" (1986:59).

INSTITUTIONAL RESPONSES

The question comes down to this: Whose hand should rock the cradle, mom and dad's or Uncle Sam's? (Dole 1989)

Secretary of Labor Elizabeth Dole's answer to the above question was unequivocal: Uncle Sam does not need to be directly involved in the business of child care. The Bush administration, like the Reagan administration before it, is caught between recognizing the plight of working parents and advancing its "sanctity of family life" ideology. In the United States we have customarily viewed work/family cross-pressures as essentially personal problems rather than public issues; parents have been expected to manage their own time constraints and to locate and coordinate their own child-care arrangements. In short, these are seen as problems of *individuals* (and their families) and not as *societal* concerns. From this perspective, working mothers themselves should fashion their own solutions for their own predicaments. Examples of such individual remedies are found in the homely advice offered in women's magazines, newspapers, and self-help books. Illustratively, a monthly newsletter designed for employers to distribute to their workers includes the following suggestions (*Work and Family Life* 1987):

- Choose clothes for yourself and for younger children—this avoids frantic morning searches for lost shoes and matching socks.

- Set the breakfast table the night before—a good task for the younger child.

- Keep a petty-cash fund for all those times that a child needs to take a quarter, or 60 cents, or $1.35 to school.

- If you can make the morning less rushed, you will find that you feel better and work better all day.

Such advice is arguably sound, but it cannot help but perpetuate the view that the time pressures working mothers face are, in effect, private troubles requiring private solutions. An alternative perspective, gaining increasing acceptance in the 1980s and 1990s, holds that family role overloads and strains are a consequence of the way in which work is structured in our society. Working hours as well as other employment conditions are geared to a "male as breadwinner" world, an increasingly outdated model for today's two-paycheck and single-parent families. A third position asserts that the unequal sharing of household work between men and women is an even more insidious structural constraint. Social observers with the latter two perspectives argue that we need employment policies that permit both men and women to better mesh their work and family roles, and we need a more equitable division of household labor at home. The work place policies needed include such options as flexible working hours, child care, part-time employment, parental leaves of absence, and a reduced work week that will allow parents to work fewer hours while their children are young and to move into full-time hours when their children grow older. But who should spearhead the transformation of the work place into one better suited to the needs of working parents? Growing numbers of parents would answer with one word: government (cf. Harris 1989).

Governmental Initiatives

Historically, both the federal and state governments have taken a largely "hands off" position concerning policies for working mothers and their children. Indeed, there is still no consensus among public officials—or throughout society as a whole—about the desirability of mothers of young children even being in the labor force. The fact that there is yet no major national policy on either child care or maternity-related benefits underscores the uncertainty and often deep ambivalence of Americans regarding maternal employment. This helps explain why the United States is the only industrialized nation without such family supports.[10]

Imagine, however, a country where wives and mothers are encouraged to work outside the home—where the media recast the image of women, wives, and mothers to spotlight employment as well as homemaking; where, as a result of government subsidy, high-quality low-cost day care is readily available; where equal pay for women workers is encouraged and sexual stereotypes are discounted on the job. This portrait is not a feminist's vision of utopia, but the reality of conditions at least aspired to in the United States during the throes of World War II.[11]

Prior to World War II, protective legislation imposed restrictions on the nature and hours of women's employment. Married women often were not hired at all and those who were employed typically lost their jobs when they became pregnant. During the Great Depression married women workers were frowned on, seen as taking jobs away from (breadwinning) men.

But World War II and the accompanying labor shortage encouraged quite different sentiments. For example, a Women's Bureau publication promoted standards for maternity care, suggesting that "some women who are pregnant or who have young children may find it necessary to work."[12] Still, the maternity leave that was offered during this period was typically unpaid and was mandatory for a period of months.

World War II also witnessed the enactment of the Lanham Act of 1942, which provided matching grants to states for day-care centers to foster the employment of women in war-production industries. But facilities never met the demand for day care during the war, and support for day care ceased shortly after the war's end and the return to "normalcy." [13]

Following the war the only day-care subsidies available were provided by Head Start, a program which was begun in the 1960s to offer nutritious meals and early education to low-income preschoolers, but which, in fact, helped resolve the child-care problems of some working mothers. Congress passed a comprehensive child-care bill in 1971, but it was vetoed by President Nixon, who regarded the bill as harmful to the family-centered child rearing he preferred. However, Title XX of the Social Security Amendments, adopted in 1974, did provide grants to states for day-care services in order to facilitate the employment of low-income women. In 1976 a child-care tax credit, defining child care as a legitimate work-related expense, was legislated for families.

With the exception of the Child Care Act, vetoed by President Nixon in 1971, legislation affecting working women has focused on equality issues in the workplace. Legislators in the 1960s and early 1970s concentrated principally on the enactment of nondiscrimination and affirmative action laws. One such law, having wide repercussions, is the Pregnancy Discrimination Act of 1978 (Public Law 95–555). It states that "women affected by pregnancy, childbirth, or related medical conditions shall be treated the same for all employment-related purposes, including receipt of benefits under fringe benefit programs, as other persons not so affected but similar in their inability to work." If an employer generally provides disability benefits, such benefits must also be available to pregnant women. Five states (California, Hawaii, New Jersey, New York, and Rhode Island) and Puerto Rico mandate the provision of temporary disability benefits to workers. This means that approximately 40 percent of employed women in all the United States have the right to a maternity leave with partial wage replacement—usually for six weeks—at the time of childbirth. The Pregnancy Discrimination Act constitutes the only federal policy enacted expressly to provide maternity or parental leave-related benefits.

Child-care benefits for middle-income families, in the form of tax credits, were not widely available until the passage of the Economic Recovery Tax Act of 1981. The Dependent Care Tax Credit it established allows parents to deduct up to $2,400 per year for the cost of caring for one child and $4,800 for two or more children. The actual credit taken, however, depends on the amount of income earned, making it far more beneficial to middle- and upper-income families. Over seven million families claimed the Dependent Care Tax Credit in 1984, establishing it as the largest single government subsidy for child care.

Such tax credits are relatively meaningless for families with low earnings who pay little or no taxes. Moreover, the Title XX block grants to states earmarked for day care for low-income families were reduced in 1981, along with the income eligibility level necessary for families to qualify. As a result of these cutbacks, 35 states provided child-care services for fewer children in 1985 than in 1981 (AFL-CIO Executive Council 1986).

We as a nation have yet to reach a clear consensus concerning the desirability or social utility of having mothers of young children work outside the home. But demographic trends in maternal employment have captured the public interest, and the dilemmas of working parents became a major policy issue in the 1980s. The first federal parental-leave bills—mandating job-protected time off for either parent following childbirth or adoption—were introduced into Congress in 1985, and in 1990 Congress passed the Family and Medical Leave Act, which was subsequently vetoed by President Bush. The introduction and reintroduction of child-care bills providing grants to states and to the private sector to expand and improve child care have sparked a new debate on the federal role in child care. In 1987 the Supreme Court, in a landmark decision, upheld a California law requiring employers to give female workers an unpaid pregnancy disability leave of up to four months with a guarantee that their jobs will be available when they return to work. The provision of separate treatment on the basis of pregnancy or childbirth-related disabilities was a result.

These issues have also been joined by a growing number of states. In the 1970s Montana, Connecticut, and Massachusetts and, in 1980, California passed maternity leave legislation. In 1987 Minnesota enacted the first parental-leave law in the nation, enabling each parent to take up to six weeks of unpaid leave following the birth or adoption of a child. Subsequently, a number of other states passed maternity or parental-leave laws.[14] Clearly, work/family concerns have become firmly established as public issues.

These issues are addressed, in part, as welfare issues. Despite the provision of transfer payments in the form of Aid for Dependent Children (AFDC), the economic plight of single-parent mothers and their children has been a growing cause for alarm (Bergmann and Roberts 1987; Folbre 1987). Child care has long been linked to social welfare programs. The Title XX Social Services Block Grant, for example, was targeted specifically to low-income families; however, as part of the growing dissatisfaction with the current welfare strategy has come a recognition of the importance of maternal employment. Consequently, legislators increasingly couch welfare reform in terms of employment and see child-care responsibilities as impediments to the economic self-sufficiency of women raising children on their own. As Christopher Dodd, the Senate Democratic sponsor of a major day-care bill concludes:

We can afford to have child care because the absence of it is costing so much. We're paying out $10 billion a year in [welfare] payments to start with, and any survey done that I've seen in the last decade or so indicates that the major reason why people do not get off welfare and go to work is the absence of any kind of child-care program. (Noble 1988)

One of the most conservative senate Republicans, Orrin Hatch, well illustrates the bipartisan approach to child care. After first sponsoring a child-care bill of his own, Senator Hatch agreed to become a cosponsor of the Dodd bill. These actions are evidence of a growing acceptance in the halls of Congress of some form of public support for child care, at least for poor children whose parents now lack the means to purchase child care in the open market.

Both parental leaves of absence and child care have been very much on the front burner at both the federal and state levels, with coalitions of child-care advocates, women's and professional groups, and unions actively lobbying for their preferred bills. Both major party presidential candidates prominently featured child care in their 1988 campaigns. The Republican and Democratic political parties actively wooed the group labeled TICKS (two-income couples with kids). With over half the mothers of infants and over two-thirds of the mothers of dependent children now in the labor force, working family concerns are not going to disappear from the policy agenda.

Few politicians quarrel with the notion that parents—or at least new mothers—require some time off following the birth of a child or with the need for expanded and improved child-care arrangements. But still to be resolved are such critical issues as whether parental leaves should be mandated by the federal government and, if so, how long such leaves should last, who should be eligible, whether they should be paid or unpaid, and how to apportion the costs that inevitably accrue to businesses offering these leaves.

Similarly, conservative and liberal legislators alike are coming to terms with the child-care dilemma. Increasingly, the issue is not whether affordable, quality child care should be available but what role the federal government should play in its provision and regulation.

Government as Employer. As the nation's largest employer, the federal government can serve as both an innovator of enlightened personnel policies and a model for the private as well as the public sector to emulate. Two pieces of legislation enacted in 1978 granted to federal employees greater discretion in fashioning their working hours. Public Law 95–347 encourages part-time employment, especially "career" part-time employment for workers who desire less than full-time hours on the job. Following a favorable evaluation of a three-year experiment with flexible work schedules by the Office of Personnel Management, Congress enacted Public Law 95–390, which provides the option of "flexitime" in all federal agencies. With this encouragement, almost one-fourth of all federal workers now work on flexible schedules. A 1987 establishment survey found that almost two in five (38%) federal, state, and local government agencies reported having flexitime policies. Although this was lower than the proportion of private industry establishments with flexitime (44%), these government agencies were far more likely (26%

versus 10%) to have employer-sponsored day care than were private sector establishments (Bureau of Labor Statistics 1988).

But government policies may inhibit as well as promote changes in employment conditions that would help workers with young children resolve their time pressures. For example, certain fixed labor costs, such as premiums for unemployment and disability insurance, make two part-time workers more expensive to employ than one full-time worker. And wage-and-hour laws require the payment of overtime rates beyond the eight-hour day, which discourages flexibility in arranging work time. Federal laws, then, sometimes work at cross-purposes, inadvertently impeding innovations in the way work—and the life course—is structured.

Employer Initiatives

Although the private sector has generally been slow to respond to the changes in the work force, private sector initiatives, at least among large corporations, are on the move. Employers have been adopting new personnel policies and benefits for three reasons: (1) to attract and retain workers in a tight labor market, (2) to enhance productivity and reduce absenteeism, and (3) to be socially responsible in the eyes of the public. These work and family initiatives take a number of forms: creating or subsidizing child-care facilities and services; providing information, counseling, and referral services; offering financial assistance for child care; easing rigid time demands; contributing to community child-care programs; and facilitating the geographical relocation of workers and their families.[15] Government encouragement in the form of tax incentives is no small inducement to act, as is the threat of government intervention through mandating benefits. However, employers, individually and through their trade associations, argue that changes in employment conditions and benefits should remain voluntary and not be imposed by federal or state governments. For example, both the U.S. Chamber of Commerce and the National Association of Manufacturers have vigorously attacked the parental-leave bills introduced in Congress on the grounds that, if enacted, such legislation would be excessively costly, prohibitively so to small businesses. Their opposition remains strident despite the fact that none of the bills introduced would apply to employers of fewer than fifteen workers and that the General Accounting Office (1988) estimates that such leaves would entail only modest costs for companies. The employer position is well stated by Alexander B. Trowbridge, president of the National Association of Manufacturers:

Employers, not government, are in the best position to decide the type and scope of benefits to be made available to employees. The economic feasibility of parental leave programs is different for each company. It is determined by a wide range of factors, including the type of business, competitive standards in the industry, the size and skill of the workforce, and the company's ability to assume costs. Such factors must be taken into account when planning benefits packages. (Bureau of National Affairs 1987:A-14)

There is little systematically gathered and nationally representative trend data on the numbers and types of firms offering flexible working hours, parental leave, and child-care assistance. But the existing evidence suggests that it is the larger businesses that are taking the lead in adopting work/family policies, with these initiatives accelerating in the 1980s and 1990s. Moreover, family supportive personnel policies and benefits are most likely to be adopted by firms with larger numbers of young, female, skilled, and nonunion workers, as well as those imbued with a strong sense of social responsibility.[16]

But the driving force impelling change typically is more pragmatic than philosophical. As John Bell, senior vice-president of the Bank of America, said, "Corporations will change when it is in their interest to do so" (Bohen 1983:33). It appears that this self-interest is beginning to surface. Growing numbers of firms are now in the process of reexamining and changing their employment practices. Large trend-setting corporations, such as IBM, Kodak, Xerox, and Corning, are developing particularly comprehensive, wide-ranging family-supportive policies for their employees. But these changes are themselves uneven, and most small companies and many large ones have yet to adopt new policies. The following sections describe some of the most significant innovations made to date in the private sector.

Child Care. Employer assistance for child care can range from the establishment and financial support of on-site day-care centers to information about and referral to services available within the community. Since the information and referral option is the least costly, not surprisingly it is the most prevalent—and expanding—form of employer assistance. A 1987 Bureau of Labor Statistics survey of business establishments revealed that only about 2 percent (25,000) of the nation's establishments with ten or more employees provided day-care centers for their workers' children, but that 11 percent provided some form of child-care assistance, ranging from counseling and information and referral to actual employer-sponsored day care.[17] The study also found that larger, private sector establishments as well as government agencies were the most likely to provide these supports. (In 1981 Congress made the provision of child care a nontaxable benefit, encouraging firms to include it as an option in flexible benefit plans.)

Historically, the provision of child-care services has been contingent on the demand for women workers. During World War II, for example, war plants such as Kaiser Shipbuilding Corporation in Portland, Oregon, operated day care centers, but they disappeared at the war's end with demobilization and the departure of mothers of young children from the labor force. In the 1970s only a few industry-sponsored child-care facilities were in operation. However, by the 1980s, the proliferation of working mothers spurred new interest. Still, even progressive corporations like IBM and Kodak prefer not to get directly involved in the child-care business, although they recognize the need to provide some kind of child-care assistance (Women's Bureau 1971, 1983).

Part-Time Employment. Part-time employment has been—and remains—a popular strategy for managing work/family cross-pressures while children are young. Wives and mothers who constitute the bulk of the part-time and temporary work force are described by the president of Manpower Inc., one of the country's largest temporary worker agencies, as "people with one foot in the house and one foot in the workplace" (Serrin 1986).

Many employers are reluctant to create part-time jobs because of the extra costs involved in recruiting and training due to turnover and in benefit provisions. As described by one bank official: "Our experience with part-time work has not been all that good. Our turnover rates are enormous. This means that by the time they are trained they are gone—and all that experience goes down the drain" (Axel 1985:28).

Work at Home. Some observers see working at home as a way of simultaneously handling work and family roles, an arrangement encouraged by new technologies for data processing and electronic communication. The "flexible work site" alternative is an increasingly popular choice among some professionals; the number of Americans working at home has grown from 24.9 million in 1988 to 38.4 million in 1991 (Evans 1991). However, this option is not always feasible—it certainly is not available in all jobs—and it may present problems. For example, in 1978 Continental Illinois Bank initiated a project in which word processing was done at home and transmitted to the central office by telephone; however, the bank aborted this trial program in 1982 because it was far more costly than had been anticipated. In some instances, one in-house staff person was needed for nearly each home operator (Axel 1985:30).

The current discussion of "homework" is reminiscent of the ideological and political debate on labor regulation that took place during the 1930s and 1940s. To the more traditionally minded, such as Alabama's Senator Denton and Utah's Senator Hatch, who concede the family's need for two incomes but believe mothers should care for their own children, homework is viewed as an ideal arrangement. But its opponents see it as a step backward, in that it reinforces the traditional sexual division of labor (Boris 1986). Most unions strongly oppose homework because of its potential for the exploitation of workers, the difficulty in enforcing labor standards laws, and the impediments it presents to organizing efforts (Christensen 1987). Survey data reveal that fewer than one in ten establishments (8%) offered any work-at-home options in 1987.

Job Sharing. Having two employers share a single job, like working at home, is another widely discussed but infrequently adopted innovation, an option offered to any employees in only 15.5 percent of business establishments (Bureau of Labor Statistics 1988). Job sharing typically permits two employees to divide the responsibilities of a full-time job by working part-time hours but with regular employee status and prorated benefits. However, this option requires (1) a job that can be logically split into separate but interrelated assignments, (2) two compatible and highly motivated workers, and (3) a supervisor who can cope with the exigencies of the arrangement. Job sharing is usually initiated by employees rather than their managers and is usually established on an individual rather than on a company-wide basis (Olmstead and Smith 1983; Axel 1985).

Flexitime. Flexibility in the scheduling of working hours is continuing to gain popularity among employers and workers alike—but not for the same reasons—with over two-fifths of establishments now offering flexitime arrangements (Bureau of Labor Statistics 1988). Employers are motivated to adopt flexitime—generally offering limited discretion in arrival or departure times—primarily to maximize the use of capital equipment or to extend the time available for customer service, not to address work/family considerations. Since its inception in the United States in the early 1970s, the adoption of flexitime has grown fairly rapidly; by 1985 about 12 percent of all full-time workers were on some kind of flexible work schedule.[18]

Flexible Time Off. Because workers who are also mothers of young children often use "sick leave" time to deal with family matters, many employers have adopted a "personal days off" policy, permitting workers to allocate a fixed block of time to vacation, sick leave, or other personal days off. This kind of flexibility is especially common in larger firms;

slightly over two-fifths of establishments with ten or more employees reported some type of flexible leave policy in 1987.[19]

Voluntary Reduced Time. Some employers allow workers to reduce their working hours temporarily on a voluntary basis when, for instance, child care and other family responsibilities require them to spend more time at home. This is a form of part-time employment, but with an important difference: In many respects the job remains full-time because it provides the employment security, status, (pro-rated) benefits, and opportunity for advancement derived from regular employment. This policy is particularly noteworthy in that it recognizes the ebb and flow of child-care responsibilities and permits parents maximum flexibility in managing the competing agendas of their work and family lives. The Shaklee Corporation and the State Government of New York are among the numerous employers who offer this voluntary reduced (v-time) work time option. Over one-third (34.8%) of the establishments surveyed in 1987 reported that they provide some form of a voluntary part-time option (Bureau of Labor Statistics 1988).

Parental Leaves. A 1988 survey conducted by the Bureau of Labor Statistics found that only 2 percent of the full-time employees in mid-size to large firms had paid maternity leave and only 1 percent had paid paternity leave available. However, one-third of those surveyed reported that they were able to take unpaid maternity leave and 16 percent could take unpaid paternity leave, each for an average of four months.[20]

Relocation Support. "Trailing spouses" present particular problems for firms that commonly relocate their employees. Workers in the 1980s began to balk at transfers, even those involving promotions, that would disrupt their spouses' employment and their families' community ties. As a consequence, corporations have been encouraged to adopt policies to facilitate such moves, such as providing assistance in locating new jobs for spouses. A 1986 survey of working parents found that fewer than one in five (17%) had employers who offered job counseling and job finding services to spouses when relocating (Opinion Research Corporation 1987).

Union and Labor-Management Initiatives

I can hear them now: What's an official of a macho male coal miners' union doing in a place like this? (Stephen F. Webber, United Mine Workers of America, Testimony at Congressional Hearing on Parental and Disability Leave, October 1985)

Unions historically have fought for improvements in wages and job security as their top priorities before turning to such "peripheral" issues as child care and maternity leave. However, with benefits a progressively larger portion of the total compensation package, family-related concerns are becoming an increasingly important bargaining issue.[21]

Being represented by a union does not necessarily increase the likelihood of receiving family benefits. For example, a study conducted by labor economists Richard Freeman and James Medoff (1984) found that—given similar companies, work forces, and economic and social conditions—union members were *less* likely than unrepresented workers to be eligible for maternity leave with pay. On the other hand, they were *more* likely to have maternity leave with full return rights and *more* likely to have day care as a fringe benefit. [22]

Given the major influx of women into labor unions, as well as the general decline in the organized segment of the work force, family support issues are likely to become more prominent at the bargaining table and in organizing campaigns. Moreover, the provision of greater flexibilities in the time structure of work may be more negotiable than the size of the total wage package in an era of economic adversity, marked by wage cutbacks and layoffs.[23]

UNMET NEEDS

More than 100 bills in Congress, hundreds of major newspaper, magazine and trade publication articles, dozens of studies and surveys both scholarly and popular, and a variety of organized forums have clearly communicated widespread concern that a crisis exists and is spreading in the ability of America's parents to find care for their children. (U.S. Department of Labor 1988:1)

The work/family connection has now conspicuously entered the policy arena, but neither public nor private sector policies have kept pace with the changing demography of the labor force. Workers need a *range* of options—parental leaves, temporarily reduced work weeks, flexitime, family and personal leave time for the care of children—for those periods of the life course when family demands are particularly acute. All of these options are feasible in the United States and many are being adopted by the largest, most progressive corporations. But none of them are in widespread practice.

As government, business, and labor tackle the challenge of meshing work and family roles, two life course considerations emerge. The first is that working mothers, or more generally working parents, of young children constitute only a minority of the work force at any one point in time. Although most workers eventually become parents, comparatively few have young children concurrently. This fact necessarily raises an equity question: Should parents of young children be alloted a disproportionately large share of the benefit pie? One solution to the equity problem is a flexible benefits plan that, within standard financial limits, permits workers to select those benefits that best meet their individual and family needs. Given these options, some workers may well choose child-care subsidies; others may elect more vacation time, enhanced retirement benefits, or extended health coverage. Another, at least partial, solution is to fold child care into the larger domain of dependent care. Although not everyone must provide care for preschool children, most workers have or can expect to have aging parents or other relatives or disabled family members who will require, at some time, their time and attention.

A second life course issue concerns the typical career trajectory of most jobs. Taking time out of the labor force or even working a reduced schedule while one's children are young can wreak havoc on long-term occupational achievement. For example, a job sharer at Michigan State University speaks of her career as "on hold" and concedes, "I'm not going to go anywhere in a half-time job and I know that" (Apgar 1985). What is required are life course solutions that offer greater flexibility in the scheduling of working hours and greater variability in the paths leading to long-term occupational goals. Everyone need not march in lock step through life, progressing from education to employment and ultimately to leisure (in the form of retirement) in a fixed order and schedule. Rather, innovative policies permitting time off and reduced work time in the child-rearing years could introduce greater flexibility and creativity in structuring education, work, and free time throughout the life course. These arrangements can not only help meet the needs of working parents but also contribute to the creation of the more flexible and adaptable work force required by the economy.

Three interrelated concerns are central to contemporary discussions of the economic scene in the United States: flexibility, productivity, and competitiveness. Experts generally acknowledge that greater flexibility in the organization of work can enhance productivity and that productivity is the key to improving America's competitive position in the world economy. This premise may be good news for women trying to combine work and family roles since "flexibility" is their watchword as well. And, to be sure, a number of firms in the 1980s adopted policies permitting much greater flexibility in the allocation of time, thereby easing the strains on working parents.

But the reality is that most women and, hence, the majority of working mothers, are employed in small firms which are the least likely to consider alternative employment policies and practices. Furthermore, many midsize and large firms, rather than initiate innovative changes, tend to react to government exhortations or the prospect of legislative mandates. For example, in a 1984 survey, over half the sample of the largest U.S. corporations reported changing their parental leave policies within the last five years, largely in response to the Pregnancy Discrimination Act (Catalyst 1986). Still, only about two-fifths of working women receive any kind of maternity benefits with even partial wage replacement for six to eight weeks (Kamerman and Kahn 1986). In the absence of government encouragement and regulation, private sector supports for working parents seem destined to remain uneven and to offer only minimal assistance to the majority of workers.

NOTES

1. The new jobs created have been disproportionately oriented to women, considering that they traditionally have been employed in service-type jobs (Oppenheimer 1970).

2. For a discussion of part-time workers, see Belous (1989), International Labour Organization (1989), and Kahne (1985).

3. Clearly, women are found in an expanding range of occupations. Nevertheless, there has been little change in the gender composition of many major occupational groups. In 1960, 28 percent of all women workers held jobs that were at least 90 percent female. By 1980 a *higher* proportion—32 percent—were in such "occupational ghettos" (Reskin and Hartmann 1986). There has been far more occupational segregation in part-time employment than in full-time jobs (Holden and Hansen 1987).

4. A number of scholars have tackled this question (e.g., Bergmann 1986, 1989; Bielby and Baron 1986; Coverman 1987; Fuchs 1988; Hartmann 1976, 1987; Jacobs 1989; Reskin 1988; Reskin and Hartmann 1986; Reskin and Roos 1990; Strober and Arnold 1987).

5. Employers and unions as well as workers are finding it difficult to continue to partition the family and the work place into two discrete domains (see reports by Bohen 1983; Bureau of National Affairs 1984, 1986; Catalyst 1986; Friedman 1986a, 1986b; Galinsky 1987).

6. Several studies confirm this tendency (Almquist, Angrist, and Mickelsen 1980; Hertz 1987; Mortimer, Hall, and Hill 1978; Presser 1989).

7. See Desai, Leibowitz and Waite (1989), Moen (1985, 1989), and Sorensen (1983).

8. About 6 percent of the working mothers interviewed in a Census Bureau survey conducted in 1984–85 reported that either they or their spouse had lost time at work during the previous month because of problems with their child-care arrangements (U.S. Bureau of the Census 1987; see also Corcoran and Duncan 1979; Dickenson 1975; Fuchs 1988; Leigh 1983; Saltford and Heck 1989).

9. Working mothers in a 1985 study of five large "technically oriented" firms spoke of missed days at work, leaving work early or arriving late, and spending "unproductive" time at work because of their preoccupation with child-care problems or other conflicting role obligations. Almost three-fourths of the women surveyed—whether married or single—reported that their dual work and family responsibilities created stress for them at work. Similar proportions of single-parent fathers recounted such stress, but only a minority of married men reported stress related to child care and balancing work and family roles. Nearly half the working mothers of preschoolers in the study said they might consider quitting their jobs because of child-care problems (Fernandez 1986; see also Friedman 1986a; Saltford and Heck 1989).

10. Several authors offer a comparative perspective: Kamerman, Kahn, and Kingston (1983), Kamerman and Kahn (1988), Gladstone, Williams, and Belous (1985), and Moen (1989).

11. Aspired to but not achieved. Campbell (1984) reports that work by mothers of young children was highly controversial and not encouraged, and that the day care was of indifferent to mediocre quality.

12. U.S. Department of Labor (1942), cited in Gladstone, Williams, and Belous (1985).

13. See discussions of this period (Campbell 1984; Kaledin 1984; Margolis 1984; Milkman 1987; Tobias and Anderson 1974).

14. For a discussion of the effects of state maternity leave statutes, see Trzcinski (1990, 1989). States having maternity or parental-leave law legislation at the time of this writing are Connecticut, Iowa, Louisiana, Maine, Minnesota, Oregon, Rhode Island, Tennessee, Washington, West Virginia, and Wisconsin (Finn-Stevenson and Trzcinski 1990).

A few local governments also have addressed the work/family predicament. In California, for example, the cities of Concord and San Francisco imposed in 1985 a small fee on commercial developments within the city and earmarked these funds for child care (Lydenberg 1986).

15. Bureau of National Affairs (1984, 1986), Friedman (1986a, 1986b), and Axel (1985).

16. See Axel (1985). Some national surveys of large corporations and select response rates suggest that there was about a fourfold increase (to 2,500) in the first half of the 1980s in the number of companies helping with their employees' child-care needs (Friedman 1986a).

17. Less than 2 percent (18,048) of the private industry establishments surveyed sponsored day-care centers, and 3 percent (34,968) provided financial assistance for child care.

18. A companion concept of flexitime is the compressed work week, which usually allows employees to put in forty hours in a four-day rather than a five-day period. Compressed working hours may be popular with some segments of the work force but typically not with working parents, who can not put child-care responsibilities "on hold" for four long working days. It is estimated that fewer than 3 percent of the labor force were working a compressed workweek schedule in 1980 (Axel 1985).

19. See Axel (1985) and Kamerman and Kahn (1986). Data come from the Bureau of Labor Statistics (1988).

20. The trend line in the provision of maternal or parental leaves remains open to question. A 1980–81 survey of various sized firms found about half offered some form of maternity disability leave (Kamerman, Kahn, and Kingston 1983). A 1984 survey of some of the nation's largest corporations found that fully 95 percent of the companies responding offered some form of paid disability leave. However, since only about one-fourth (26%) of the corporations contacted returned the questionnaire, it is likely that those responding were more apt to offer these benefits. Even within this select sample, employers were far less supportive of leaves for new fathers than for new mothers; almost two-thirds considered it unreasonable for men to take any amount of parental leave (Catalyst 1986). For a fuller discussion of parental-leave policies at the state level see Trzcinski (1990).

21. See Foner (1980, 1987) and Needleman and Tanner (1987). In 1951, fringe benefits accounted for less than 19 percent of total payroll costs; by 1982, this had risen to almost 37 percent. By 1983, maternity leave provisions were included in over one-third (36%) of the collective bargaining agreements. By comparison, more than three-fourths of the contracts provided for military leave (76%) and personal leave (75%) (Gladstone, Williams, and Belous 1985).

22. See also Freeman and Leonard (1987).

23. The innovative policies on flexible schedules, voluntary furloughs, and on-site day care adopted through negotiations between New York State and the unions representing its employees stand as an example of what can be accomplished through the collaborative efforts of management and labor, and they point to the leadership role that can be assumed by unions in easing the burdens of working parents (Bureau of National Affairs 1984, 1986).

III New Directions

6 CONCLUSIONS AND IMPLICATIONS

As a nation, we have two choices. One is to continue to let our biases dominate our behavior as a society. The other is to see that we are a nation in crisis.

(Brazelton 1989:70)

WOMEN WITH CHILDREN LAST

The statistics are remarkable: The number of women in the labor force has tripled over the last forty years, and the proportion of working mothers of young children has more than quadrupled. American women have been entering employment since before the turn of the century, but only during the last twenty years has the employment of mothers of preschoolers—and now mothers of infants—become commonplace. Today most husbands have working wives, most children have working mothers, and almost half the work force is female. This extraordinary social transformation has had profound repercussions on every facet of American society. Yet our basic institutions—family, work, government, school—have only begun to respond to this fundamental reconfiguration of women's lives.

The United States is not unique in facing the dilemma of women's two roles, but it *is* unique in its reluctance to join the issue in the policy arena. Why this is so can be ascribed to societal ambivalence about "working" mothers. We fiercely defend the sanctity of home and family. Having mothers of young children take on paid work seems to threaten the very foundation of our nostalgic vision of family life. Moreover, mandating private supports to working parents is seen as infringing on the free enterprise system and as detrimental to business interests. Either private or public supports would represent a value statement, in effect endorsing maternal employment, something many Americans are still reluctant to do.

In the United States traditional life patterns presume that families have a full-time homemaker (or some surrogate) when the children are small. Employers do not see workers as encumbered with family responsibilities. Schools, dentists, and physicians arrange schedules that assume someone (a mother) is available to accompany children to appointments and to care for them before and after school, on vacations, and on "snow days." Until recently, these conventional institutional arrangements have not been challenged because women have taken on two jobs—at home and at work—thereby minimizing the disruptions in either domain. Now, however, the sheer number of working mothers is straining the system of patchwork arrangements devised by individual women, individual families.

THE BALANCE SHEET: COSTS VERSUS BENEFITS

While we have found the continuing upward trend in women's employment—and especially the employment of mothers of young children—to be simple and straightforward, the implications of this trend—for women, for men, and for children—are far from simple or straightforward. We have seen that the employment of women who are mothers has undeniably led to beneficial outcomes. It has broadened women's options and has promoted their self-esteem and their economic independence. In addition to facilitating their own career development, the movement of women into the labor force has created opportunities for future generations of women. Through employment, women are beginning to access the economic and psychic resources previously confined largely to men. To be sure, the mental and physical health costs and benefits of employment remain somewhat ambiguous, especially for mothers of young children, but the existing evidence suggests that the payoffs of employment typically outweigh the costs, and that the ratio of benefits to costs has become more favorable over time.

Husbands may be disadvantaged in the short run, but they stand to gain in the long run as the burden of breadwinning and the satisfactions of child care come to be shared and as they come to endorse their wives' employment. In addition, children can see their mothers as well as their fathers engaged in productive, socially valued activities. The national economy also benefits by acquiring the skills, talents, and productive capability of the female half of the population.

Progressive changes in the labor force participation of women have also led to major shifts in public opinion. The ideology of gender equality may not yet be firmly established, but popular conceptions of men's and women's roles are increasingly egalitarian.

Still, we found that the growth in the employment of mothers of young children has not been without its downside. Time has become the new scarcity in American family life. Employment means that mothers have fewer hours in the day or week to spend alone or with their children and their husbands. Child care has become a perennial problem. And what children need most—a stable, predictable environment—is increasingly hard to arrange. In fact, it appears that unpredictability and inconsistency increasingly characterize the daily life of American children.

Inconsistency typifies American women's lives as well. Contemporary women, like women in the 1950s, still receive contradictory messages. Now as then the problem originates in the discrepancies built into the role expectations of women. When women began to combine employment with the mothering of young children, the cross-pressures in women's lives intensified. These cross-pressures are also experienced by husbands and children as time becomes a scarce commodity.

Given well-entrenched employment policies and the traditional cultural expectation that women are responsible for the domestic work of society, most working mothers must fashion their own ways of managing these cross-pressures. The solution for most women continues to be one of accommodating work to family—in their choice of occupations, in their hours of employment, in allowing family responsibilities to constrain their work lives. A 1989 poll of working mothers conducted in the Washington, D.C., area revealed that a majority (62%) said that they would give up their jobs if they could afford it (Evans 1991). Working mothers of young children in the United States are walking a tightrope, and their balancing act is daunting.

MAXIMIZING CHOICE

In making the new versions of the old understandings, people naturally rely on what they already have available, so that consciously planned innovations and revolutions seem, in historical perspective, only small variations on what came before. (Becker 1981:20)

In contemporary society, industry establishes the rhythm of life. Employment timetables program and largely preempt our waking hours. The predicament for families—especially those with children—is that they possess their own rhythms, their own timetables. An infant demands to eat—and possibly even to play—at three in the morning, despite the fact that both parents must go to work only a few hours later. Or a three-year-old falls from a slide in the afternoon and requires emergency medical care that cannot be put off until after working hours.

The issue, then, is not only the scarcity of time in contemporary family life but also its management. Most employment by its very nature is bureaucratic, necessitating ordered, fixed schedules. Family life by its nature is nonbureaucratic, requiring flexible, ever-changing, and often unanticipated tasks and timetables. When both parents (or single parents) are employed, trying to fit family life into the windows of free time (that is, time not allocated to work) is a formidable struggle.

Balancing the demands of work and family is a Herculean task for which, unfortunately, success in one domain often means failure in the other. As economist Victor Fuchs points out, it is a task "most men have never even tried" let alone accomplished (Fuchs 1988:61; also see Oakley 1974).

What options are available? We have seen that the solution to the competing time demands of work and family in the United States in the years immediately following World War II was the one that had worked before the war for those who could afford it: the full-time housewife. Women's domestic labor as full-time wives and mothers enabled husbands and fathers to concentrate almost exclusively on their jobs and facilitated the smooth functioning of the market economy. Thus, the postwar "feminine mystique" was a celebration of domesticity, encouraging women to devote themselves full-time to their families, at least until their children left home. Is this arrangement possible today?

The "Traditional Family" Solution

Theoretically, returning to a traditional, gender-based division of labor might be possible, but only if government were to provide the economic supports, such as a children's allowance, necessary to permit one parent (or the single parent) to remain at home. Given current budget problems, the prospect of comprehensive government programs to support families with children seems remote.

The reality is that most families require two incomes to make ends meet. The movement of wives and mothers into the labor force reflects at least in part the declining real wages of husbands and fathers, concomitant with escalating costs and the quest for a higher standard of living.

Beyond these family financial needs, we must also consider women's spiraling occupational aspirations. Increasing education, growing acceptance of gender equality, declining fertility, delays in marriage and motherhood—all point to life plans in which paid work figures prominently. Given the increasing probability of divorce and single-parenthood, women look to their own employment for financial security. And women increasingly see the costs—to their careers, wages, and seniority—of the old system of sequencing work before and after the child-rearing years.

The traditional two-parent, single-earner family will be a viable option but for an ever-smaller segment of women who can afford to be full-time homemakers and who prefer this life-style. In the postwar 1950s, most American women, unlike men, could choose whether to enter or to remain in the labor force. In the 1990s, the evidence suggests that exclusive homemaking is no longer a viable option for most women, even during the child-rearing years.

The "Male Model" Solution

At the other end of the choice spectrum is the possibility for women to emulate men's life patterns, by taking on full-time continuous employment throughout adulthood. This is feasible only if government and employers take on the responsibility for providing a comprehensive program of child care, freeing women to concentrate on their jobs in the same way that women have traditionally freed men from domestic concerns. This arrangement, however, flies in the face of the deep reservations many Americans harbor about exclusively institutional child care and their enduring commitment to the traditional family.

A variant of the male model option is the pursuit of two "tracks" by women: one, like men's, aiming toward occupational success; the other accomodating work to family roles. While men could have both children at home and success at work, women would have to choose one as a priority over the other. But women electing the family track would find themselves disadvantaged in the job market. Moreover, growing numbers of women (as well as men) have called for a concept of equality that does not use men's occupational achievement as the yardstick. Betty Friedan (1981), for one, labeled the family as the "new frontier" of feminism. She and other feminists argue that family roles, no less than work roles, should be available to all women (as well as to men) regardless of their career aspirations. It is not that women have different roles to play but that parenting is patently impossible if both men and women take on the traditional male role.

The "Technological" Solution

Some propose a technological solution, with novel labor-saving devices and at-home work arrangements (i.e., "telecommuting"), to relieve the time constraints on contemporary families. Indeed, growing numbers of workers are finding ways to do their work at home. Clearly, the advent of fax machines, home computers, and desktop publishing permits greater flexibility in the time and timing, as well as location, of work. But home-based work is not a panacea. Unlike housework, child care cannot be put "on hold" for more convenient moments or simply neglected for short periods of time altogether. Still, the growth in home-based work suggests that this strategy lessens, if not resolves, the work/family dilemma for some parents.

Other technological and social inventions can prove beneficial. The proliferation of housecleaning and lawn services, fast-food chains, and prepared foods undoubtedly have reduced the domestic burden. Some feel that the establishment of (or increased support for) privately or publicly supported agencies for doing such ordinary household chores as cooking and laundering, as well as providing daytime and evening child care, would promote greater cooperation between men and women. In this way reducing the demands on women would not increase demands on their husbands.

Nevertheless, the care of children cannot be "faxed"; although most see institutionalized child care as an increasingly important necessity, especially for toddlers, Americans are reluctant to send their newborn infants out, like the laundry, to be "done" elsewhere.

The "New Man" Solution

"Changing men" is a popularly prescribed remedy today because many feminists see asymmetry in the division of household labor as an underlying cause of women's contemporary dilemma. Having husbands and fathers do more than just "help out" with housework and child care obviously would lessen the strains on working wives and mothers. As long as child care, homemaking, and a family's "emotional work" are accomplished principally by women, women will be at a decided disadvantage in the world of work.

Still, the current structure of jobs prevents men as well as women from meshing occupational requirements with family obligations. Since men, on the average, earn more than women and are not subject to gender discrimination, it has thus far "made sense" from the perspective of the household economy to have the man in the family invest most heavily in his job. Consequently, to achieve true equality in the domestic division of labor would require changing the structure of work for *both* women and men, as well as providing men with the skills, supports, and motivation to share in domestic work.

The "Life Course" Solution

In many ways this is the most radical option: to rethink and redesign not only the structure of work but also the configuration of the life course. The typical life pattern for American men has consisted of twenty or more years of schooling, forty or more years of employment, and the remaining years spent in retirement leisure. For American women, on the other hand, the prime working years have been a combination and sequencing of domestic and paid labor. As women have moved into and remain in the labor force, they have been adopting a modified version of the traditional male life course, but one that is *combined* with their continuing family responsibilities.

Rethinking the lockstep pattern of education, employment, and retirement could lead to a variety of arrangements, including a return to school at various ages and a continuation of paid work well beyond the usual age of retirement. It could also encourage both men and women to cut back on their working hours or to take extended sabbaticals while their children are young. The changes we as a society are experiencing call loudly for a thoughtful reappraisal of existing life patterns. This could lead to a reconfiguration of the life course in ways that create more options and a greater diversity for both men and women in youth, early adulthood, mid-life, and the later years.[1]

Much of the stress experienced by working mothers is a product of the time constraints imposed by their jobs. For example, part-time work has been shown to reduce the strains on women and to benefit their husbands and children; but part-time jobs in the United States typically offer few benefits and little job security, pay low wages, and entail little prospect for advancement. Still, the standard five-day, forty-hour work-week need not be considered immutable. Indeed, this "normal" work schedule dates back only to the 1930s (Harriman 1982). Employment policies offering greater flexibility in working hours, including both parental leaves of absence and a temporary reduction in working hours while children are young, could substantially alleviate the strains workers face in coping with the competing demands of work and family. It could also provide a constructive societal response to the inherent contradictions in women's two roles.

The traditional life course sequence of education–paid work–retirement grows increasingly obsolete even apart from its serving as an impediment to reconciling work and family roles. Training and retraining throughout the life course are now essential for creating a productive work force. Moreover, an aging population means that much of the nation's valued human resources are languishing in retirement. Just as government has been influential in establishing the current sequencing of roles (by legislation affecting schooling, employment, and retirement), so too must it play a major role in redesigning the life course, for example, by providing tax incentives and other encouragements to employers to give greater flexibility to employees in shaping their own work lives.

This is a radical option, but in many ways it is also a conservative one. Rearranging the life patterns of work to permit some reductions during the child-rearing years (such as parental leaves, sabbaticals, a reduced work week) would, in effect, bolster the sanctity of the family. Children would see more of their parents; family life would be less hectic; and neither parent would be forced to sacrifice career for family, or vice versa. Recasting the conventional patterning of work, education, and leisure over the life course to be more flexible could actually reinforce the traditional image of the family as the caretaker of children while, at the same time, encouraging a partnership between mothers and fathers in the sharing of both the breadwinning and care-giving roles.

THE FORCES OF CHANGE

What will destroy us is not change, but our inability to change—both as individuals and as social systems. (Otto 1970:9)

The difficulty faced by working mothers, now as in the 1950s, is that our institutions—the labor market as well as marriage—have not accommodated themselves to women's changing roles. Why is this recalcitrance especially true in the United States? In the first chapter we presented three realities that preclude a national commitment to resolving this impasse. The first is that this is a *transition in progress*; there is no broad consensus as to what women's (or men's) roles should be. There is considerable variation among women's life patterns and values. Many women are themselves ambivalent about their combined roles as wives, mothers, and workers. But as younger women and men, who stand at the vanguard of this social revolution, replace older generations, maternal employment may gain the same acceptance as paternal employment. These younger cohorts face a tapestry of choices and changes—in the timing of marriage and motherhood, in the number of children they bear, in the duration of their marriages, in their attitudes about gender equality, and in their educational and employment aspirations and achievements. All of these considerations make their lives decidedly different from those of previous generations, and they call for new strategies and innovations at home and at work.

A second reality lies in the *prevailing ideology* in the United States that centers on the sacredness of the family and on an inherent suspicion of government intervention. Concern about the erosion of the traditional family is mirrored in the deep-seated ambivalence most Americans have about the employment of mothers of young children. Historically, gender has defined and limited the principal role options realistically available to men and women. Responsibility for child care and homemaking has traditionally restricted women's lives. This notion of women's proper role is deeply entrenched in the belief systems and behavioral norms of American society. While it is true that growing numbers of men and women endorse employment for women generally, for wives, and for mothers of older children, women as well as men frequently express apprehension about the employment of mothers of infants and preschoolers. This attitude may reflect a realistic assessment of the impediments to managing work and parenting. Or it may be more a product of deeply held values, in which the family, as we have long known it, is seen as the very foundation of American society. Gender, after all, is a fundamental and thoroughly entrenched social marker and source of personal identity. Even in a socially progressive country like Sweden, with all its policies promoting gender equality, women still assume the bulk of child-care responsibilities (Moen 1989).

Concerns about government interference in family life has also been an enduring theme in the United States, as evidenced in President Nixon's rationale for his veto of the 1971 child-care bill. Many Americans see the family as the last bastion of personal freedom; they would regard any federal actions to facilitate the employment of mothers of young children as undermining homemaking and other traditional values. At the same time, fears about government interference in the free market system have also endured, as underscored in President Bush's rationale for his veto of the 1990 parental-leave bill.

The third reality concerns the inevitability of *structural lags*. While workplace policies may well adapt to the labor force participation of mothers of young children in time, there is a certain inertia to be overcome. Men, whether as husbands, legislators, or corporate leaders, may see little to gain and much to lose (i.e., power, prestige, resources) if institutional changes were to produce gender equality. From this perspective it is only when the employment of mothers of young children is perceived as an economic or social imperative that significant changes will be made—as they were by government in the labor shortage era of World War II, or by families when a household needs two incomes to maintain an acceptable standard of living, or by legislators as a preferred alternative to government transfer payments (i.e., welfare).

Understanding all three of these separate but interconnected realities may help us appreciate the formidable dilemma we face in the United States as a result of the spiraling numbers of working mothers. Yet there is cause for guarded optimism about the future. The evidence presented in the preceding chapters suggests that Americans' notions of the "proper" roles of men and women are changing at a rapid rate. Moreover, the declining labor supply, as a consequence of reduced fertility and the ever-earlier retirements of older workers, renders women's employment even more essential to the national economy. Also, as Helen Axel (1985) points out, in the 1990s many (male) business leaders will themselves be members or products of working-couple or single-parent families. Consequently, they are likely to be far more sensitive to the work/family overloads of their employees and more inclined to deal with them. Increasing numbers of managers will be women. When asked what would best bring about corporate policies for working parents, Dana Friedman of the Families and Work Institute replied quite simply, "A pregnant chief executive officer."

Realistically, there is most probably no single solution to the work/family dilemma. Given the diversity in women's (and men's) lives, in families, and in jobs, a smorgasbord of options and alternatives may well be necessary. Current public and political attention to the need for child care reflects a welcome acknowledgment of the plight of working families. However, it tends to invoke an essentially one-sided response. Many Americans persist in seeing the principal remedy as a change in family demands (in this case by providing child care) without altering the fundamental structure of work or the way in which we typically organize our lives. While affordable, high-quality child care is, of course, a necessary step toward a solution, it is not, by itself, a sufficient one. Equally critical, in my view, are new arrangements in the sequencing of periods of work and nonwork over the life course and in the ability to reduce hours on the job to permit mothers and fathers to *lessen their work obligations temporarily* while maintaining their job security and their career options. Parental leaves of absence and sabbaticals for an interval following the birth or adoption of a child are two such devices, as is the cutback of full-time employment to part-time schedules (without changing jobs) for a reasonable period of time during the child's early years. Other possibilities include flexible work schedules, the ability to work at home, and extended time off for the care of children. Permitting American workers to tailor their working hours—and their work lives—to their family circumstances would very likely reinforce their work commitment, enhance their work performance, and generally contribute to the development of a more productive as well as a more satisfied labor force.

In fashioning these innovative arrangements, it should be kept in mind that the period of child rearing is not long lasting. Parenthood has come to occupy only a relatively short span of time in contemporary adulthood in the United States as a result of both reduced fertility and increased longevity. Indeed, today's parents will have very young preschoolers in the home for two or three years, typically twice in their lives, while the average working life exceeds forty years. Thus, provisions for meshing working and parenting can be short term and flexible—options to be chosen as time and circumstances require.

The fundamental challenge to women—and to men—is to build a life that includes both family and work roles. The difficulty is that the child-nurturing years are also the career-nurturing years. What is lost in either case cannot be "made up" at a later time. Viable solutions to the dilemma of women's two roles must be grounded in this reality.

NOTE

1. See discussions by Best (1980), Kahne (1985), and Harriman (1982). Sweden is trying to offer such flexibilities to working parents (Moen 1989). The flexibility that new technologies are requiring of the work force—to change jobs and to be continuously trained and retrained—is comparable to that needed by workers in the early years of childbearing. See Riley and Riley (1989) for a discussion of the need to refashion the life course in light of shifts in the age composition.

BIBLIOGRAPHY

AFL-CIO Executive Council. 1986. "Resolution and Fact Sheets on Work and Family." *Daily Labor Review* 37 (February 25):E1–E6.

Aldous, Joan. 1983. *Two Paychecks: Life in Dual Earner Families.* Beverly Hills, CA: Sage.

Almquist, Elizabeth M., and Shirley S. Angrist. 1971. "Role Model Influences on College Women's Career Aspirations." *Merrill-Palmer Quarterly* 17:265–69.

Almquist, Elizabeth M., Shirley S. Angrist, and Richard Mickelsen. 1980. "Women's Career Aspirations and Achievements: College and Seven Years After." *Sociology of Work and Occupations* 7:367–84.

Alwin, Duane F., Michael Braun, and Jacqueline Scott. 1990. "The Separation of Work and Family: Gender Differences in Sex-Role Attitudes in Britain, Germany and the United States." Paper presented at the meeting of the International Sociological Society, Madrid, Spain, July.

Anderson, Karen. 1981. *Wartime Women: Sex Roles, Family Relations, and the Status of Women during World War II.* Westport, CT: Greenwood Press.

Andre, Rae. 1981. *Homemakers: The Forgotten Workers.* Chicago: University of Chicago Press.

Andrews, F. M., and S. B. Withey. 1976. *Social Indicators of Well-Being: Americans Perceptions of Life Quality.* New York: Plenum Press.

Aneshensel, Carol S., Ralph R. Frerichs, and Virginia A. Clark. 1981. "Family Roles and Sex Differences in Depression." *Journal of Health and Social Behavior* 22:379–93.

Aneshensel, Carol S., Carolyn M. Rutter, and Peter A. Lachenbruch. 1991. "Social Structure, Stress, and Mental Health: Competing Conceptual and Analytic Models." *American Sociological Review* 56:166–78.

Angrist, Shirley S., and Elizabeth M. Almquist. 1975. *Careers and Contingencies: How College Women Juggle with Gender*. New York: Dunellen.

Apgar, Leonard M. 1985. "Labor Letter." *Wall Street Journal*, July 30.

Astin, Alexander W., Kenneth C. Green, and William S. Korn. 1987. *The American Freshman: Twenty Year Trends, 1966–1985*. Los Angeles: University of California, Higher Education Research Institute.

Astin, Alexander W., Kenneth C. Green, William S. Korn, Merilyn Schalit, and Ellync R. Berz. 1989. *The American Freshman: National Norms for Fall 1988*. Los Angeles: University of California, Higher Education Research Institute.

Axel, Helen. 1985. *Corporations and Families: Changing Practices and Perspectives*. Research Report No. 608. New York: The Conference Board.

Axelson, Leland J. 1963. "The Marital Adjustment and Marital Role Definitions of Husbands of Working and Nonworking Wives." *Marriage and Family Living* 24:189–95.

Bahr, S. J. 1974. "Effects on Power and Division of Labor in the Family." In *Working Mothers*, edited by Lois W. Hoffman and F. Ivan Nye. San Francisco: Jossey Bass.

Banducci, R. 1967. "The Effect of Mother's Employment on the Achievement, Aspirations, and Expectations of the Child." *Personnel and Guidance Journal* 46:263–67.

Bane, Mary Jo, Laura Lein, Lydia O'Donnell, C. Ann Strieve, and Barbara Wells. 1979. "Child Care Arrangements of Working Parents." *Monthly Labor Review* 102:50–56.

Banner, Lois. 1974. *Women in Modern America: A Brief History*. New York: Harcourt Brace Jovanovich.

Barglow, P., B. E. Vaughn, and N. Molitor. 1987. "Effects of Maternal Absence due to Employment on the Quality of Infant-Mother Attachment in a Low-Risk Sample." *Child Development* 58:945–54.

Barnett, Rosalind C., and Grace K. Baruch. 1985. "Women's Involvement in Multiple Roles and Psychological Distress." *Journal of Personality and Social Psychology* 49:135–45.

Barrett, Nancy. 1979. "Women in the Job Market: Occupations, Earnings, and Career Opportunities." In *The Subtle Revolution*, edited by Ralph E. Smith. Washington, DC: Urban Institute.

Baruch, Grace K. 1972. "Maternal Influence upon College Women's Attitudes towards Women and Work." *Developmental Psychology* 6:32–37.

———. 1984. "The Psychological Well-Being of Women in the Middle Years." In *Women in Midlife*, edited by Grace K. Baruch and Jeanne Brooks-Gunn. New York: Plenum Press.

Baruch, Grace K., and Rosalind C. Barnett. 1986a. "Consequences of Fathers' Participation in Family Work: Parents' Role Strain and

Well-Being." *Journal of Personality and Social Psychology* 51:983–92.

———. 1986b. "Role Quality, Multiple Role Involvement, and Psychological Well-Being in Mid Life Women." *Journal of Personality and Social Psychology* 51:578–85.

———. 1987. "Role Quality and Psychological Well-Being." In *Spouse, Parent, Worker: On Gender and Multiple Roles*, edited by Faye J. Crosby. New Haven, CT: Yale University Press.

Baruch, Grace K., Rosalind C. Barnett, and C. Rivers. 1984. *Lifeprints: New Patterns of Love and Work for Today's Women*. New York: Signet.

Baruch, Grace K., Lois Biener, and Rosalind C. Barnett. 1987. "Women and Gender in Research on Work and Family Stress." *American Psychologist* 42:130–36.

Becker, Gary. 1981. *A Treatise on the Family*. Cambridge, MA: Harvard University Press.

Belkin, Lisa. 1989. "Bars to Equality of Sexes Seen As Eroding, Slowly." *New York Times*, August 20.

Belle, Deborah, ed. 1982. *Lives in Stress: Women and Depression*. Beverly Hills, CA: Sage.

Belous, Richard S. 1989. *The Contigent Economy: The Growth of the Temporary, Part-Time and Subcontracted Workforce*. Washington, DC: National Planning Association.

Belsky, Jay. 1986. "Infant Day Care: A Cause for Concern?" *Zero to Three* 6:1–6.

———. 1987a. "The "Effects" of Infant Day Care Reconsidered." *Early Childhood Research Quarterly* 7:1–69.

———. 1987b. "Science, Social Policy and Day Care: A Personal Odyssey." Paper presented at the biennial meeting of the Society for Research in Child Development. Baltimore, Maryland, April.

Belsky, Jay, and Michael J. Rovine. 1988. "Nonmaternal Care in the First Year of Life and the Security of Infant-Parent Attachment." *Child Development* 59:157–67.

Belsky, Jay, Richard M. Lerner, and Graham B. Spanier. 1984. *The Child in the Family*. Reading, MA: Addison-Wesley.

Belsky, Jay, and L. D. Steinberg. 1978. "The Effects of Day-Care: A Critical Review." *Child Development* 49:929–49.

Bergmann, Barbara R. 1986. *The Economic Emergence of Women*. New York: Basic Books.

———. 1989. "Does the Market for Women's Labor Need Fixing?" *Journal of Economic Perspectives* 3:43–60.

Bergmann, Barbara R., and Mark D. Roberts. 1987. "Income for the Single Parent: Child Support, Work, and Welfare." Pp. 247–70 in *Gender in the Workplace*, edited by Clair Brown and Joseph A. Pechman. Washington, DC: Brookings Institution.

Berk, Richard A., and Sarah Fenstermaker Berk. 1979. *Labor and Leisure at Home*. Beverly Hills, CA: Sage.

———. 1983. "Supply-Side Sociology of the Family: The Challenge of the New Home Economics." *Annual Review of Sociology* 9:373–95.

Berk, Sarah Fenstermaker 1985. *The Gender Factory: The Apportionment of Work in American Households*. New York: Plenum Press.

Berkin, Carol R., and Clara M. Lovett, eds. 1980. *Women, War, and Revolution*. New York: Holmes and Meier.

Bernard, Jessie. 1972. *The Future of Marriage*. New York: Bantam.

———. 1974. *The Future of Motherhood*. New York: Penguin.

———. 1981. "The Good Provider Role: Its Rise and Fall." *American Psychologist* 36:1–12.

Best, Fred. 1980. *Flexible Life Scheduling: Breaking the Education-Work-Retirement Lockstep*. New York: Praeger.

Bianchi, S. M., and Daphne Spain. 1986. *American Women in Transition*. New York: Russell Sage.

Bielby, Denise Del Vento. 1978. "Career Sex-Atypicality and Career Involvement of College Educated Women: Baseline Evidence from the 1960s." *Sociology of Education* 51:7–28.

Bielby, Denise Del Vento, and William T. Bielby. 1984. "Work Commitment, Sex-Role Attitudes, and Women's Employment." *American Sociological Review* 49:234–47.

Bielby, William T., and James Baron. 1986. "Women and Work: Sex Segregation and Statistical Discrimination." *American Journal of Sociology* 91:759–99.

Bielby, William T., and Denise Del Vento Bielby. 1989. "Family Ties: Balancing Commitments to Work and Family in Dual Earner Households." *American Sociological Review* 54:776–89.

Birnbaum, Judith A. 1975. "Life Patterns and Self-Esteem in Gifted Family Oriented and Career Committed Women." In *Women and Achievement: Social and Motivational Analyses*, edited by Martha T. S. Mednick, Sandra S. Tangri, and Lois W. Hoffman. Washington, DC: Hemisphere.

Blau, David M., and Philip K. Robins. 1989. "Fertility, Employment and Child-Care Costs." *Demography* 26:287–300.

Blau, Francine D., and Marianne A. Ferber. 1986. *The Economics of Women, Men, and Work*. Englewood Cliffs, NJ: Prentice Hall.

Blood, Robert O., Jr. 1963. "The Husband-Wife Relationship." In *The Employed Mother in America*, edited by F. I. Nye and L. W. Hoffman. Chicago: Rand McNally.

Blood, Robert O., Jr., and Donald M. Wolfe. 1960. *Husbands and Wives*. Glencoe, IL: Free Press.

Bohen, Halcyone H. 1983. *Corporate Employment Policies Affecting Families and Children: The United States and Europe*. New York: Aspen Institute.

Bolger, Niall, Anita DeLongis, Ronald C. Kessler, and Elaine Wethington. 1989. "The Contagion of Stress across Multiple Roles." *Journal of Marriage and the Family* 51:175-83.

————. 1990. "The Microstructure of Daily Role-related Stress in Married Couples." In *Stress between Work and Family*, edited by John Eckenrode and Susan Gore. New York: Plenum Press.

Booth, Alan. 1977. "Wife's Employment and Husband's Stress: A Replication and Refutation." *Journal of Marriage and the Family* 39:645-50.

————. 1979. "Does Wives' Employment Cause Stress for Husbands?" *Family Coordinator* 28:445-50.

Booth, Alan, D. R. Johnson, and L. Whyte. 1984. "Women, Outside Employment, and Marital Instability." *American Journal of Sociology* 90:567-83.

Boris, Eileen. 1986. " 'Right to Work' as a 'Women's Right': The Debate over the Vermont Knitters, 1980-1985." *Legal History Program Working Papers* 1(5):1-54.

Bose, Christine E. 1984. "Household Resources and U.S. Women's Work: Factors Affecting Gainful Employment at the Turn of the Century." *American Sociological Review* 49:474-90.

Bott, Elizabeth. 1957. *Family and Social Network: Roles, Norms, and External Relationships in Ordinary Urban Families*. London: Tavistock.

Boyle, Maureen. 1989. "Spending Patterns and Income of Single and Married Parents." *Monthly Labor Review*, March, 37-41.

Bradburn, Norman, and D. Caplovitz. 1965. *Report on Happiness*. Chicago: Aldine.

Brazelton, T. Berry. 1989. "Working Parents." *Newsweek*, February 13, 66-70.

Brim, Orville G., Jr., and Jerome Kagen, eds. 1980. *Constancy and Change in Human Development*. Cambridge, MA: Harvard University Press.

Bronfenbrenner, Urie. 1982. "The Context of Development and the Development of Context." Pp. 1-64 in *Developmental Psychology: Historical and Philosophical Perspectives*, edited by R. M. Lerner. Hillsdale, NJ: Erlbaum.

————. 1991. "Child Care in the Anglo-Saxon Mode." In *Nonparental Childcare: Cultural and Historical Perspectives*, edited by M. Lamb, K. Sternberg, C. Hwang, and A. Broberg. Hillsdale, NJ: Elbaum (in press).

————. 1992. *On Making Human Beings Human*. Cambridge, MA: Harvard University Press (in preparation).

Bronfenbrenner, Urie, W. F. Alvarez, and C. R. Henderson, Jr. 1984. "Working and Watching: Maternal Employment Status and Parents' Perceptions of Their Three-Year-Old Children." *Child Development* 55:1362-78.

Bronfenbrenner, Urie, and Ann Crouter. 1982. "Work and Family through Time and Space." In *Families That Work: Children in a Changing*

World, edited by Sheila B. Kamerman and C. D. Hayes. Washington, DC: National Academy Press.

Brown, George W., and T. Harris. 1978. *Social Origins of Depression*. New York: Free Press.

Bryant, F. B., and J. Veroff. 1982. "The Structure of Psychological Well-Being: A Sociohistorical Analysis." *Journal of Personality and Social Psychology* 43:653–73.

Bureau of Labor Statistics. 1985. *News*. USDL 85–355. Washington, DC: U.S. Department of Labor.

————. 1986. "Half of Mothers with Children under 6 Now in Labor Force." *News*. USDL 86–345. Washington, DC: U.S. Department of Labor.

————. 1988. "BLS Reports on Employer Child-Care Practices." *News*. USDL 88. Washington, DC: U.S. Department of Labor.

————. 1989. "Employment and Earnings Characteristics of Familes: Second Quarter 1989." *News*. USDL 89–368. Washington, DC: U.S Department of Labor.

Bureau of National Affairs. 1984. *Employers and Child Care: Development of a New Employee Benefit*. Washington, DC: Bureau of National Affairs.

————. 1986. *Work and Family: A Changing Dynamic*. Washington, DC: Bureau of National Affairs.

————. 1987 *Daily Labor Report*. Washington, DC: Bureau of National Affairs.

————. 1989. *The 1990s Father: Balancing Work and Family Concerns*. Washington, DC: Bureau of National Affairs.

Burke, R., and S. Weir. 1976. "Relationships of Wives' Employment Status to Husband, Wife and Pair Satisfaction and Performance." *Journal of Marriage and the Family* 38:279–87.

Burr, Wesley R., Geoffrey K. Leigh, Randall D. Day, and John Constantine. 1979. "Symbolic Interaction and the Family." In *Contemporary Theories about the Family*, vol. 2, edited by W. R. Burr, R. Hill, F. I. Nye, and I. L. Reiss. New York: John Wiley and Sons.

Cain, Glen G. 1966. *Married Women in the Labor Force: An Economic Analysis*. Chicago: University of Chicago Press.

Cain, Virginia S., and Sandra L. Hofferth. 1989. "Parental Choice of Self-Care for School-Age Children." *Journal of Marriage and the Family* 51:65–78.

Campbell, Angus. 1982. "Changes in Psychological Well-Being during the 1970's of Homemakers and Employed Wives." In *Women's Lives: New Theory, Research and Policy*, edited by Dorothy G. McGulgan. Ann Arbor: University of Michigan, Center for Continuing Education of Women.

Campbell, Angus, Philip E. Converse, and Willard L. Rodgers. 1976. *The Quality of American Life: Perceptions, Evaluations, and Satisfactions*. New York: Russell Sage.

Campbell, D'Ann. 1984. *Women at War with America: Private Lives in a Patriotic Era.* Cambridge, MA: Harvard University Press.

Catalyst. 1986. *Report on a National Study of Parental Leaves.* New York: Catalyst.

Chafe, William. 1972. *The American Woman: Her Changing Social, Economic, and Political Roles, 1920–1970.* New York: Oxford University Press.

Chafetz, Janet S., and Anthony G. Dworkin. 1986. *Female Revolt: Women's Movements in World and Historical Perspective.* Totowa, NJ: Rowman and Allanheld.

Chase-Lansdale, P. Lindsay, and Margaret Tresch Owen. 1987. "Maternal Employment in a Family Context: Effects on Infant-Mother and Infant-Father Attachments." *Child Development* 58:1505–12.

Cherlin, Andrew. 1980. "Postponing Marriage: The Influence of Young Women's Work Expectations." *Journal of Marriage and the Family* 42:355–65.

———. 1981. *Marriage, Divorce, and Remarriage: Changing Patterns in the Post War United States.* Cambridge, MA: Harvard University Press.

Cherlin, Andrew, and Pamela Barnhouse Walters. 1981. "Trends in United States Men's and Women's Sex-Role Attitudes: 1972–1978." *American Sociological Review* 46: 453–60.

Cherry, F. F., and E. L. Eaton. 1977. "Physical and Cognitive Development in Children of Low-Income Mothers Working in the Child's Early Years." *Child Development* 48:158–66.

Chion-Kenny, Linda. 1988. "Another Way to Have It All." *Washington Post,* May 31, C5.

Christensen, Kathleen E. 1987. "Women, Families, and Home-Based Employment." In *Families and Work,* edited by Naomi Gerstel and Harriet Engel Gross. Philadelphia: Temple University Press.

Clarke-Stewart, K. Alison. 1977. *Child Care in the Family.* New York: Academic Press.

———. 1989. "Infant Day Care: Maligned or Malignant?" *American Psychologist* 44:266–73.

Clausen, John A. 1986. *The Life Course: A Sociological Perspective.* Englewood Cliffs: Prentice Hall.

Cleary, Paul, and David Mechanic. 1983. "Sex Differences in Psychological Distress among Married People." *Journal of Health and Social Behavior* 24:111–21.

Cohen, Patricia, Jim Johnson, Selma A. Lewis, and Judith S. Brook. 1990. "Single Parenthood and Employment: Double Jeopardy?" In *Stress between Work and Family,* edited by John Eckenrode and Susan Gore. New York: Plenum Press.

Cohn, Samuel. 1985. *The Process of Occupational Sex-Typing.* Philadelphia: Temple University Press.

Corcoran, M., and Greg J. Duncan. 1979. "Work History, Labor Force Attachment and Earnings Differences between Races and Sexes." *Journal of Human Resources* 14:3–20.

Coser, Rose L., and Gerald Rokoff. 1971. "Women in the Occupational World: Social Disruption and Conflict." *Social Problems* 18:535–54.

Cott, Nancy F., and Elizabeth H. Pleck, 1979. *A Heritage of Her Own: Toward a New Social History of American Women.* New York: Simon and Schuster Press.

Coverman, Shelley. 1985. "Explaining Husbands' Participation in Domestic Labor." *Sociological Quarterly* 26:81–97.

———. 1987. "Sociological Explanations of the Male-Female Wage Gap: Individualist and Structuralist Theories." In *Women Working*, 2d ed., edited by A. Stromberg and S. Harkess. Mountain View, CA: Mayfield.

Coverman, Shelley, and Joseph F. Sheley. 1986. "Change in Men's Housework and Child-Care Time, 1965–1975." *Journal of Marriage and the Family* 48:413–22.

Cowan, Alison Leigh. 1989. "Women's Gains on the Job: Not without a Heavy Toll. *New York Times*, August 21.

Cowan, Ruth Schwartz. 1983. *More Work for Mother.* New York: Basic Books.

Cramer, James C. 1980. "Fertility and Female Employment: Problems of Causal Direction." *American Sociological Review* 45:167–90.

Crosby, Faye J., ed. 1987. *Spouse, Parent, Worker: On Gender and Multiple Roles.* New Haven, CT: Yale University Press.

Crouter, Ann C. 1984. "Spillover from Family to Work: The Neglected Side of the Work Family Interface." *Human Relations* 37:425–42.

Crouter, Ann C., Jay Belsky, and Graham Spanier. 1984. "The Family Context of Child Development." In *The Annals of Child Development*, edited by G. Whitehurst. Greenwich, CT: JAI Press.

Crouter, Ann C., Maureen Perry-Jenkins, Ted L. Huston, and Susan M. McHale. 1987. "Processes Underlying Father Involvement in Dual-Earner and Single-Earner Families." *Developmental Psychology* 23:431–40.

Daniels, Pamela, and Kathy Weingarten. 1982. *Sooner or Later: The Timing of Parenthood in Adult Lives.* New York: W. W. Norton.

Davis, Kingsley. 1984. "Wives and Work: The Sex Role Revolution and Its Consequences." *Population and Development Review* 10:397–417.

Davis, Kingsley, and Pietronella Van den Oever. 1982. "Demographic Foundations of New Sex Roles." *Population and Development Review* 8:495–511.

Degler, Carl N. 1980. *At Odds: Women and the Family in America from the Revolution to the Present.* New York: Oxford University Press.

DeMeis, Debra K., Ellen Hock, and Susan L. McBride. 1986. "The Balance of Employment and Motherhood: Longitudinal Study of Mothers'

Feelings about Separation from Their First-Born Infants." *Developmental Psychology* 22:627–32.

Desai, Sonalde, P. Lindsay Chase-Lansdale, and Robert T. Michael. 1989. "Mother or Market? Effects of Maternal Employment on the Intellectual Ability of 4-Year-Old Children." *Demography* 26:545–61.

Desai, Sonalde and Linda Waite. 1991. "Women's Employment During Pregnancy and after the First Birth: Occupational Characteristics and Work Commitment." *American Sociological Review* 56:551–566.

Dickenson, Katherine. 1975. "Child Care." In *Five Thousand American Families: Patterns of Economic Progress*, Vol. 3 edited by Greg J. Duncan and James N. Morgan. Ann Arbor: University of Michigan, Institute for Social Research.

Dizard, J. 1968. *Social Change in the Family*. Chicago: University of Chicago, Community and Family Study Center.

Dole, Elizabeth. 1989. "Statement by Secretary of Labor Elizabeth Dole." *News*. USDL 89–310. June 22. Washington, DC: U.S. Department of Labor.

Downey, Geraldine, and Phyllis Moen. 1987. "Personal Efficacy, Income and Family Transitions: A Longitudinal Study of Women Heading Households." *Journal of Health and Social Behavior* 28:320–33.

Duncan, Beverly, and Otis Dudley Duncan. 1978. *Sex Typing and Social Roles: A Research Report*. New York: Academic Press.

Duncan, Greg, and C. Russell Hill. 1975. "Modal Choice in Child Care Arrangements." In *Five Thousand American Families: Patterns of Economic Progress*, vol. 3, edited by Greg J. Duncan and James N. Morgan. Ann Arbor: Survey Research Center, Institute for Social Research.

———. 1977. "The Child Care Mode Choice of Working Mothers." In *Five Thousand American Families: Patterns of Economic Progress*, vol. 5, edited by Gary J. Duncan and James N. Morgan. Ann Arbor: Survey Research Center, Institute for Social Research.

Easterbrooks, M. A., and W. A. Goldberg. 1988. "Security of Toddler-Parent Attachment: Relation to Children's Socio-Personality Functioning during Kindergarten." In *Attachment in the Preschool Years: Theory, Research, and Intervention*, edited by M. Greenberg, D. Cicchetti, and M. Cummings. Chicago: University of Chicago Press.

Eckenrode, John, and Susan Gore. 1990. "Stress and Coping at the Boundary of Work and Family." Pp. 1–17 in *Stress between Work and Family*, edited by John Eckenrode and Susan Gore. New York: Plenum Press.

Eckenrode, John, and Susan Gore, eds. 1990. *Stress between Work and Family*. New York: Plenum Press.

Elder, Glen H., Jr. 1975. "Age Differentiation and the Life Course." *Annual Review of Sociology* 1:165–90.

———. 1985. *Life Course Dynamics: Trajectories and Transitions, 1968–1980*. Ithaca, NY: Cornell University Press.

Elkind, David. 1981. *The Hurried Child: Growing up Too Fast Too Soon.* New York: Addison-Wesley.

Emmons, Carol-Ann, Monica Biernat, Linda Beth Tiedje, Eric L. Lang, and Camille B. Wortman. 1990. "Stress, Support, and Coping among Women Professionals with Preschool Children." Pp. 61–94 in *Stress between Work and Family*, edited by John Eckenrode and Susan Gore. New York: Plenum Press.

England, Paula, and George Farkas. 1986. *Households, Employment and Gender: A Social Economic and Demographic View.* New York: Aldine.

Ericksen, J. A., W. L. Yancey, and E. P. Ericksen. 1979. "The Division of Family Roles." *Journal of Marriage and the Family* 42:301–14.

Espenshade, T. J. 1985. "Marriage Trends in America: Estimates, Implications, and Underlying Causes." *Population and Development Review* 11:193–245.

Evans, Sara. 1991. "For Many Mothers, Home Is Where the Office Is." *Washington Post*, June 21.

Evans, Sara M. 1989. *Born for Liberty: A History of Women in America.* New York: Free Press.

Farkas, George. 1976. "Education, Wage Rates, and the Division of Labor between Husband and Wife." *Journal of Marriage and the Family* 46:871–79.

Farley, Reynolds. 1984. *Blacks and Whites: Narrowing the Gap?* Cambridge, MA: Harvard University Press.

Faver, Catherine A. 1984. *Women in Transition: Career, Family and Life Satisfaction in Three Cohorts.* New York: Praeger.

Feld, S. 1963. "Feelings of Adjustment." In *The Employed Mother in America*, edited by F. Ivan Nye and Lois W. Hoffman. Chicago: Rand McNally.

Felmlee, Diane H. 1984. "A Dynamic Analysis of Women's Employment Exits." *Demography* 21:171–83.

Fernandez, John P. 1986. *Child Care and Corporate Productivity: Resolving Family/Work Conflicts.* Lexington, MA: Lexington Books.

Ferree, Myra Marx. 1976. "Working-Class Jobs: Housework and Paid Work as Sources of Satisfaction." *Social Problems* 23:431–41.

———. 1987. "Family and Job for Working-Class Women: Gender and Class Systems Seen from Below." Pp. 289–301 in *Families and Work*, edited by Naomi Gerstel and Harriet Engels Gross. Philadelphia: Temple University Press.

Finn-Stevenson, Matia, and Eileen Trzcinski. 1990. "Public Policy Issues Surrounding Parental Leave: A State-by-State Analysis of Parental Leave Legislation" (Unpublished draft).

Floge, Liliane. 1985. "The Dynamics of Child Care Use and Some Implications for Women's Employment." *Journal of Marriage and the Family* 47:143–54.

———. 1989. "Changing Household Structure, Child-Care Availability, and Employment among Mothers of Preschool Children." *Journal of Marriage and the Family* 51:51–64.

Folbre, Nancy. 1987. "The Pauperization of Motherhood: Patriarchy and Public Policy in the United States." Pp. 491–511 in *Families and Work*, edited by Naomi Gerstel and Harriet Engels Gross. Philadelphia: Temple University Press.

Foner, Philip S. 1980. *Women and the American Labor Movement: From World War I to the Present*. New York: Free Press.

———. 1987. "Women and the American Labor Movement: A Historical Perspective." Pp. 154–86 in *Working Women: Past, Present, Future*, edited by Karen Shallcross Koziara, Michael H. Moskow, and Lucretia Dewey Tanner. Washington, DC: Bureau of National Affairs.

Freeman, Richard B., and Jonathan S. Leonard. 1987. "Union Maids: Unions and the Female Work Force." Pp. 189–216 in *Gender in the Workplace*, edited by Clair Brown and Joseph A. Pechman. Washington, DC: Brookings Institution.

Freeman, Richard B., and James L. Medoff. 1984. *What Do Unions Do?* New York: Basic Books.

Friedan, Betty. 1963. *The Feminine Mystique*. New York: W. W. Norton.

———. 1981. *The Second Stage*. New York: W. W. Norton.

Friedman, Dana E. 1986a. "Child Care for Employees' Children." *Harvard Business Review* 64:28–32.

———. 1986b. *Families and Work: Managing Related Issues*. New York: The Conference Board.

Fuchs, Victor R. 1988. *Women's Quest for Economic Equality*. Cambridge, MA: Harvard University Press.

Galinsky, Ellen. 1987. "Corporate Policies and Family Life." In *Stresses and Supports for Families*, edited by M. Yogman and T. Brazelton. Boston: Harvard University Press.

Gallese, Liz Roman. 1989. "Corporate Women on the Move." *Business Month*, April, 31–56.

Garfinkel, Irvin, and Sara McLanahan. 1986. *Single Mothers and Their Children: A New American Dilemma*. Washington, DC: Urban Institute.

Gavron, Hannah. 1966. *The Captive Wives: Conflicts of Housebound Mothers*. London: Routledge and Kegan Paul.

Gecas, Victor. 1976. "The Socialization and Child Care Roles." In *Role Structure and Analysis of the Family*, edited by F. Ivan Nye. Beverly Hills, CA: Sage.

Geerken, Michael, and Walter R. Gove. 1983. *At Home and at Work: The Family's Allocation of Labor*. Beverly Hills, CA: Sage.

General Accounting Office. 1988. *Parental Leave: Estimated Cost of Revised Parental and Medical Leave Act*. GAO/HRD-88-103. Washington, DC: General Accounting Office.

Gerson, Kathleen. 1985. *Hard Choices: How Women Decide about Work, Career, and Motherhood.* Berkeley, CA: University of California Press.

————. 1987. "How Women Choose between Employment and Family: A Developmental Perspective." In *Families and Work,* edited by Naomi Gerstel and Harriet Engels Gross. Philadelphia: Temple University Press.

Giele, Janet Z. 1982. "Women's Work and Family Roles." Pp. 115–50 in *Women in the Middle Years,* edited by Janet Z. Giele. New York: Free Press.

Gilder, George. 1986. *Men and Marriage.* Gretna, LA: Pelican Press.

Gillespie, D. L. 1971. "Who Has the Power? The Marital Struggle." *Journal of Marriage and the Family* 33:445–58.

Gladstone, Leslie W., Jennifer Williams, and Richard S. Belous. 1985. *Maternity and Parental Leave Policies: A Comparative Analysis.* Congressional Research Service Rep. No. 85–148 G Gov, July 16. Washington, DC: U.S. Government Printing Office.

Glenn, Norval, and Charles N. Weaver. 1978. "A Multivariate, Multisurvey Study of Marital Happiness." *Journal of Marriage and the Family* 40:269–81.

Gold, D., and D. Andres. 1978a. "Comparisons of Adolescent Children with Employed and Unemployed Mothers." *Merrill-Palmer Quarterly* 24:243–54.

————. 1978b. "Developmental Comparisons between Ten-Year-Old Children with Employed and Nonemployed Mothers." *Child Development* 49:75–84.

Gold, D., D. Andres, and J. Glorieux. 1979. "The Development of Francophine Nursery School Children with Employed and Nonemployed Mothers." *Canadian Journal of Behavioral Science* 11:169–73.

Goldberg, W. A., and M. A. Easterbrooks. 1988. "Maternal Employment When Children Are Toddlers and Kindergartners." In *Maternal Employment and Children's Development: Longitudinal Research,* edited by A. E. Gottfried and A. W. Gottfried. New York: Plenum Press.

Goldin, Claudia. 1983. "The Changing Economic Role of Women: A Quantitative Approach." *Journal of Interdisciplinary History* 23(4):707–33.

Goode, William I. 1960. "A Theory of Role Strain." *American Sociological Review* 25:483–96.

Gordon, Henry A., and Kenneth C. W. Kammeyer. 1980. "The Gainful Employment of Women with Small Children." *Journal of Marriage and the Family* 42:327–36.

Gore, S., and T. Mangione. 1983. "Social Roles, Sex Roles, and Psychological Distress: Additive and Interactive Models of Sex Differences." *Journal of Health and Social Behavior* 24:300–12.

Gottfried, A. E., and A. W. Gottfried, eds. 1988. *Maternal Employment and Children's Development: Longitudinal Research.* New York: Plenum Press.

Gove, Walter R. 1972. "The Relationship between Sex Roles, Marital Status, and Mental Illness." *Social Forces* 51:34–44.

Gove, Walter R., and Michael R. Geerken. 1977. "The Effect of Children and Employment on the Mental Health of Married Men and Women." *Social Forces* 56:66–76.

Gove, Walter R., and M. Hughes. 1979. "Possible Causes of the Apparent Sex Differences in Physical Health: An Empirical Investigation." *American Sociological Review* 44:126–46.

Gove, Walter R., and C. Peterson. 1980. "An Update of the Literature on Personal and Marital Adjustment: The Effect of Children and the Employment of Wives." *Marriage and Family Review* 3:63–96.

Gove, Walter R., and Jeanette F. Tudor. 1973. "Adult Sex Roles and Mental Illness." *American Journal of Sociology* 78:812–35.

Gove, Walter R., and Carol Zeiss. 1987. "Multiple Roles and Happiness." In *Spouse, Parent, Worker: On Gender and Multiple Roles*, edited by Faye J. Crosby. New Haven, CT: Yale University Press.

Hall, D. T. 1972. "A Model of Coping with Role Conflict: The Role Behavior of College Educated Women." *Administrative Quarterly* 17:471–89.

Harriman, Ann. 1982. *The Work/Leisure Trade Off.* New York: Praeger.

Harris, Louis. 1989. *The Philip Morris Companies Inc. Family Survey II: Child Care.* New York: Philip Morris Companies, Inc.

Hartmann, Heidi. 1976. "Capitalism, Patriarchy and Job Segregation by Sex." *Signs*: 187–171.

―――. 1981. "The Family as a Locus of Gender, Class and Political Struggle: The Example of Housework." *Signs* 6:366–94.

―――. 1987. "Internal Labor Markets and Gender: A Case Study of Promotion." In *Gender in the Workplace*, edited by Clair Brown and Joseph A. Pechman. Washington, DC: Brookings Institution.

Hayes, Cheryl D., and Sheila B. Kamerman, eds. 1983. *Children of Working Parents: Experiences and Outcomes.* Washinton, DC: National Academy Press.

Hayghe, Howard. 1978. "Marital and Family Characteristics of Workers, March 1977." *Monthly Labor Review* 101:41–54.

―――. 1981. "Husbands and Wives as Earners: An Analysis of Family Data." *Monthly Labor Review* 104:46–59.

―――. 1986. "Rise in Mothers' Labor Force Activity Includes Those with Infants." *Monthly Labor Review* 109:43–45.

―――. 1988. "Employers and Child Care: What Roles Do They Play?" *Monthly Labor Review* 111:38–44.

―――. 1990. "Family Members in the Work Force." *Monthly Labor Review* 113:14–19.

―――. 1991. Personal Communication. January.

Haynes, Suzanne G., and Manning Feinleib. 1980. "Women, Work and Coronary Heart Disease: Prospective Findings from the Framingham Heart Study." *American Journal of Public Health* 70:133–41.

Herman, J. B., and K. K. Gyllstrom. 1977. "Working Men and Women: Inter- and Intra-Role Conflict." *Psychology of Women Quarterly* 1:319–33.

Hernandez, Donald J. 1992. *America's Children since the Great Depression* New York: Russell Sage Foundation.

Hertz, Rosanna. 1986. *More Equal than Others: Women and Men in Dual-Career Marriages.* Berkeley: University of California Press.

———. 1987. "Three Careers: His, Hers, and Theirs." Pp. 408–21 in *Families and Work*, edited by Naomi Gerstel and Harriet Engels Gross. Philadelphia: Temple University Press.

Herzog, A. Regula, and Jerald G. Bachman. 1975. *Sex Role Attitudes among High School Seniors.* Ann Arbor: University of Michigan, Institute for Social Research.

Herzog, A. Regula, Jerald G. Bachman, and Lloyd Johnston. 1983. "Paid Work, Child Care, and Housework: A National Survey of High School Seniors' Preferences for Sharing Responsibilities between Husband and Wife." *Sex Roles* 9:109–35.

Heyns, Barbara. 1982. "The Influence of Parents' Work on Children's School Achievement." In *Families That Work: Children in a Changing World*, edited by Sheila B. Kamerman and Cheryl D. Hayes. Washington, DC: National Academy Press.

Heyns, Barbara, and Sophia Catsambis. 1986. "Mothers' Employment and Childrens' Achievement: A Critique." *Sociology of Education* 59:140–51.

Hill, C. Russell, and Frank P. Stafford. 1974. "Allocation of Time to Preschool Children and Educational Opportunity." *Journal of Human Resources* 9:323–41.

———. 1980. "Parental Care of Children: Time Diary Estimates of Quality, Predictability and Variety." *Journal of Human Resources* 15: 219–39.

Hochschild, Arlie. 1983. *The Managed Heart.* Berkeley: University of California Press.

———. 1989. *The Second Shift.* New York: Viking.

Hock, Ellen. 1978. "Working and Nonworking Mothers With Infants: Perceptions of Their Careers, Their Infants' Needs, and Satisfaction With Mothering." *Developmental Psychology* 14:37–43.

———. "Working and Nonworking Mothers and Their Infants: A Comparative Study of Maternal Caregiving Characteristics and Infant Social Behavior." *Merrill Palmer Quarterly* 26:79–101.

Hock, Ellen, and D. DeMeis. 1990. "Depression in Mothers of Infants: The Role of Maternal Employment." *Developmental Psychology* 26:285–91.

Hofferth, Sandra L. 1979. "Day Care in the Next Decade: 1980–1990." *Journal of Marriage and the Family* 41:649–58.

———. 1985. "Updating Children's Life Course." *Journal of Marriage and the Family* 47:93–115.

Hofferth, Sandra L., and Deborah A. Phillips. 1987. "Child Care in the United States, 1970 to 1995." *Journal of Marriage and the Family* 49:559–71.

Hoffman, Lois W. 1961. "Effects of Maternal Employment on the Child." *Child Development* 32:187–97.

———. 1963a. "Mother's Enjoyment of Work and Effects on the Child." *The Employed Mother in America*, edited by F. Ivan Nye and Lois W. Hoffman. Chicago: Rand McNally.

———. 1963b. "Parental Power Relations and the Division of Household Tasks." In *The Employed Mother in America*, edited by F. Ivan Nye and Lois W. Hoffman. Chicago: Rand McNally.

———. 1972. "Early Childhood Experiences and Women's Achievement Motives." *Journal of Social Issues* 28:129–56.

———. 1975. "The Employment of Women, Education, and Fertility." In *Women and Achievement: Social and Motivational Analyses*, edited by M.T.S. Mednick, S. S. Tangri, and L. W. Hoffman. Washington, DC: Hemisphere.

———. 1979. "Maternal Employment: 1979." *American Psychologist* 34:859–65.

———. 1984. "Work Family and the Socialization of the Child." In *Review of Child Development Research: The Family*, vol. 7, edited by Ross D. Parker. Chicago: University of Chicago Press.

———. 1987. "The Effect on Children of Maternal and Paternal Employment." In *Families and Work*, edited by Naomi Gerstel and Harriet Engel Gross. Philadelphia: Temple University Press.

———. 1989. "Effects of Maternal Employment in the Two-Parent Family." *American Psychologist* 44:283–92.

Hoffman, Lois W., and F. Ivan Nye. 1974. *Working Mothers*. San Francisco: Jossey Bass.

Holahan, C. K., and Lucia A. Gilbert. 1979. "Conflict between Major Life Roles: Women and Men in Dual Career Couples." *Human Relations* 32:451–67.

Holden, Karen C., and W. Lee Hansen. 1987. "Part-Time Work, Full-Time Work, and Occupational Segregation." In *Gender in the Workplace*, edited by Clair Brown and Joseph A. Pechman. Washington, DC: Brookings Institution.

Hood, Jane C., and S. Golden. 1979. "Beating Time/Making Time." *Family Coordinator* 28:575–82.

Howenstein, L. S., S. V. Kask, and E. Harburg. 1977. "Work Status, Work Satisfaction, and Blood Pressure among Married Black and White Women." *Psychology of Women Quarterly* 1:334–49.

Howes, Carollee. 1988. "Relations between Early Child Care and Schooling." *Developmental Psychology* 24:53–57.

Howes, Carollee, and Michael Olenick. 1986. "Family and Child Care Influences on Toddler's Compliance." *Child Development* 57:202–16.

Huber, Joan, and Glenna Spitze. 1980. "Considering Divorce: An Expansion of Becker's Theory of Marital Instability." *American Journal of Sociology* 86:75–89.

———. 1981. "Wife's Employment, Household Behaviors and Sex-Role Attitudes." *Social Forces* 60:150–69.

———. 1983. *Sex Stratification: Children, Housework, and Jobs.* New York: Academic Press.

Iglehart, A. P. 1979. *Married Women and Work: 1957 and 1976.* Lexington, MA: D. C. Heath.

International Labour Organization. 1989. *Part-Time Work. Conditions of Work Digest*, vol. 8.N.1. Geneva: International Labour Organization.

Jacobs, Jerry A. 1989. *Revolving Doors: Sex Segregation and Women's Lives.* Stanford, CA: Stanford University Press.

Johansen, A., A. Leibowitz, and L. Waite. 1988. "Child Care and Children's Illness." *American Journal of Public Health* 78:1175–77.

Johnston, Lloyd D., Jerald G. Bachman, and Patrick M. O'Malley. 1986. *Monitoring the Future: Questionnaire Responses from the Nation's High School Seniors.* Ann Arbor: University of Michigan Press.

Johnston, William B., and Arnold Packer. 1987. *Workforce 2000: Work and Workers for the 21st Century.* Indianapolis: Hudson Institute.

Juster, F. Thomas. 1985. "A Note on Recent Changes in Time Use." In *Time, Goods, and Well-Being*, edited by F. Thomas Juster and Frank P. Stafford. Ann Arbor: University of Michigan, Institute for Social Research.

Kahne, Hilda. 1985. *Reconceiving Part-Time Work: New Perspectives for Older Workers and Women.* Totowa, NJ: Rowman and Allanheld.

Kaledin, Eugenia. 1984. *Mothers and More: American Women in the 1950s.* Boston: Twayne.

Kamerman, Shelia B. 1980. *Parenting in an Unresponsive Society: Managing Work and Family Life.* New York: Free Press.

———. 1983. "Child-Care Services: A National Picture." *Monthly Labor Review* 106:35–39.

Kamerman, Sheila B., and Cheryl D. Hayes, eds. 1982. *Families That Work: Children in a Changing World.* Washington, DC: National Academy Press.

Kamerman, Sheila B., and Alfred J. Kahn. 1979. "The Day Care Debate: A Wider View." *The Public Interest* 54:76–93.

———. 1986. "Private Sector Social Policy Responsibility." *Institute of Socioeconomic Studies Journal* 11:44–60.

————. 1988. "Social Policy and Children in the United States and Europe." In *The Vulnerable*, edited by John L. Palmer, Timothy Smeeding, and Barbara Boyle Torrey. Washington, DC: Urban Institute Press.

Kamerman, Sheila B., Alfred J. Kahn, and Paul Kingston. 1983. *Maternity Policies and Working Women*. New York: Columbia University Press.

Kandel, Denise, Mark Davies, and Victoria Raveis. 1985. "The Stressfulness of Daily Social Roles for Women: Marital, Occupational, and Household Roles." *Journal of Health and Social Behavior* 26:64–78.

Kanter, Rosabeth M. 1977. *Work and Family in the United States: A Critical Review and Agenda for Research and Policy*. New York: Russell Sage.

Katzman, David M. 1977. *Seven Days a Week: Women and Domestic Service in Industrializing America*. New York: Oxford University Press.

Keith, Pat M., and Robert B. Schafer. 1983. "Employment Characteristics of Both Spouses and Depression in Two-Job Families." *Journal of Marriage and the Family* 45:877–84.

Kelly, R. F., and P. Voydanoff. 1985. "Work/Family Role Strain among Employed Parents." *Family Relations* 34:367–74.

Kessler, Ronald C., and Paul D. Cleary. 1980. "Social Class and Psychological Distress." *American Sociological Review* 45:463–78.

Kessler, Ronald C., and James A. McRae, Jr. 1981. "Trends in the Relationship between Sex and Psychological Distress: 1957–1976." *American Sociological Review* 46:443–52.

————. 1982. "The Effects of Wives' Employment on the Mental Health of Married Men and Women." *American Sociological Review* 47:216–27.

Kingston, Paul W., and Steven L. Nock. 1987. "Time Together among Dual-Earner Couples." *American Sociological Review* 52:391–400.

Klatch, Rebecca E. 1987. *Women of the New Right*. Philadelphia: Temple University Press.

Komarovsky, Mirra. 1946. "Cultural Contradictions and Sex Roles." *American Journal of Sociology* 52:184–89.

————. 1953. *Women in the Modern World: Their Education and Their Dilemmas*. Boston: Little, Brown & Co.

————. 1962. *Blue-Collar Marriage*. New York: Vintage Books.

————. 1976. *Dilemmas of Masculinity: A Study of College Youth*. New York: W. W. Norton.

————. 1982. "Female Freshmen View Their Future: Career Salience and Its Correlates." *Sex Roles* 8:299–314.

Krause, Neal. 1984. "Employment Outside the Home and Women's Psychological Well-Being." *Social Psychiatry* 19:41–48.

Krause, Neal, and Kyria S. Markides. 1987. "Gender Roles, Illness, and Illness Behavior in a Mexican American Population." *Social Science Quarterly* 68:102–21.

Lamb, Michael, and Abraham Sagi. 1983. *Fatherhood and Family Policy.* Hillsdale, NJ: Lawrence Erlbaum Associates.

Lamm, Sandra. 1986. *Speaking Out about Child Care in New York State.* New York: Commission on Child Care.

Leibowitz, A., Linda J. Waite, and Christina Witsberger. 1988. "Childcare for Pre-Schoolers: Differences by Child Age." *Demography* 25:205–20.

Leigh, J. Paul. 1983. "Sex Differences in Absenteeism." *Industrial Relations* 22:349–61.

Lennon, Mary C. 1987. "Sex Differences in Distress: The Impact of Gender and Work Roles." *Journal of Health and Social Behavior* 28:290–305.

Leon, Carol, and Robert W. Bednarzik. 1978. "A Profile of Women on Part-Time Schedules." *Monthly Labor Review* 101:3–12.

Levinson, D. J. 1978. *The Seasons of a Man's Life.* New York: Alfred A. Knopf.

Locksley, Anne. 1980. "On the Effects of Wives' Employment on Marital Adjustment and Companionship." *Journal of Marriage and the Family* 42:337–46.

Long, Clarence. 1958. *The Labor Force under Changing Income and Employment.* Princeton, NJ: Princeton University Press.

Long, Judy, and Karen L. Porter. 1984. "Multiple Roles of Midlife Women: A Case for New Directions in Theory, Research and Policy." Pp. 109–59, in *Women in Midlife,* edited by Grace Baruch and Jeanne Brooks-Gunn. New York: Plenum Press.

Lopata, Helena. 1971. *Occupation: Housewife.* New York: Oxford University Press.

Low, Seth, and Pearl G. Spindler. 1968. *Child Care Arrangements of Working Mothers in the United States.* Washington, DC: U.S. Department of Labor, Department of Health, Education and Welfare, Women's Bureau, Employment Standards Administration, and Children's Bureau.

Lydenberg, Steven D. 1986. "Child Care Update: Business Takes First Real Steps." *Newsletter,* Council on Economic Priorities, N86-11, November, 1–6.

Macke, Anne, and William R. Morgan. 1978. "Maternal Employment, Race and Work Orientation of High School Girls." *Social Forces* 57:187–204.

McLanahan, Sara, and J. Adams. 1987. "Parenthood and Psychological Well-Being." *Annual Review of Sociology* 5:237–57.

McLanahan, Sara, and Jennifer Glass. 1985. "A Note on the Trend in Sex Differences in Psychological Distress." *Journal of Health and Social Behavior* 26:328–36.

McLaughlin, Steven D., Barbara D. Melber, John O. Billy, Denise M. Zimmerle, Linda D. Winges, and Terry R. Johnson. 1988. *The*

Changing Lives of American Women. Chapel Hill: University of North Carolina Press.

Margolis, Maxine L. 1984. *Mothers and Such: Views of American Women and Why They Changed*. Berkeley: University of California Press.

Marini, Margaret M. 1980. "Sex Differences in the Process of Occupational Attainment: A Closer Look." *Social Science Research* 9:307–61.

Marks, S. R. 1977. "Some Notes on Human Energy, Time and Commitment." *American Sociological Review* 42:921–36.

Masnick, George, and Mary Jo Bane. 1980. *The Nation's Families: 1960–1990*. Cambridge, MA: Joint Center for Urban Studies of MIT and Harvard University.

Mason, Karen O., and Larry L. Bumpass. 1975. "U.S. Women's Sex Role Ideology." *American Journal of Sociology* 80:1212–19.

Mason, Karen O., and Yu-Hsia Lu. 1988. "Attitudes toward Women's Familial Roles: Changes in the United States, 1977–1985." *Gender and Society* 2:39–57.

Mason, Karen O., John L. Czajka, and Sara Arber. 1976. "Change in U.S. Women's Sex Role Attitudes, 1964–1974." *American Sociological Review* 41:573–96.

Menaghan, Elizabeth. 1989. "Role Changes and Psychological Well-Being: Variations in Effects by Gender and Role Repertoire." *Social Forces* 67:693–714.

Menaghan, Elizabeth, and Toby L. Parcel. 1990. "Parental Employment and Family Life: Research in the 1980s." *Journal of Marriage and the Family* 52:1079–98.

Milkman, Ruth. 1987. *Gender at Work: The Dynamics of Job Segregation by Sex during World War II*. Chicago: University of Illinois Press.

Miller, Joanne, and Howard H. Garrison. 1982. "Sex Roles: The Division of Labor at Home and in the Workplace." *Annual Review of Sociology* 8:237–62.

Miller, Joanne, Carmi Schooler, Melvin L. Kohn, and Karen A. Miller. 1979. "Women and Work: The Psychological Effects of Occupational Conditions." *American Journal of Sociology* 85:66–94.

Miller, Melody, Phyllis Moen, and Donna Dempster-McClain. 1991. "Motherhood, Multiple Roles and Maternal Well-Being: Women of the 1950s." *Gender & Society* 5:565–82.

Mintz, Steven, and Susan Kellogg. 1988. *Domestic Revolutions: A Social History of American Family Life*. New York: Free Press.

Mirowsky, John II, and Catherine E. Ross. 1986. "Social Patterns of Distress." *Annual Review of Sociology* 12:23–45.

Modell, John. 1986. "Normative Aspects of American Marriage Timing since World War II." *Journal of Family History* 5:210–34.

Modell, John, and Tamara K. Hareven. 1973. "Urbanization and the Malleable Household: An Examination of Boarding and Lodging in American Families." *Journal of Marriage and the Family* 35:467–79.

Moen, Phyllis. 1985. "Continuities and Discontinuities in Women's Labor Force Participation." In *Life Course Dynamics: Trajectories and Transitions, 1968 to 1980,* edited by Glen H. Elder, Jr. Ithaca, NY: Cornell University Press.

————. 1989. *Working Parents: Transformations in Gender Roles and Public Policies in Sweden.* Madison: University of Wisconsin Press.

Moen, Phyllis, and Donna Dempster-McClain. 1987. "Employed Parents: Role Strain, Work Time and Preferences for Working Less." *Journal of Marriage and Family* 49:579–90.

Moen, Phyllis, Donna Dempster-McClain, and Robin Williams, Jr. 1989. "Social Integration and Longevity: An Event History Analysis of Women's Roles and Resilience." *American Sociological Review* 54:635–47.

————. 1992. "Successful Aging: A Life Course Perspective on Women's Multiple Roles and Health." *American Journal of Sociology* (forthcoming).

Moen, Phyllis, and Kay B. Forest. 1990. "Working Parents, Workplace Supports, and Well-Being: The Swedish Experience." *Social Psychology Quarterly* 53:117–31.

Moen, Phyllis, Edward Kain, and Glen H. Elder, Jr. 1983. "Economic Conditions and Family Life: Contemporary and Historical Perspectives." In *The High Costs of Living: Economic and Demographic Conditions of American Families.* Washington, DC: National Academy of Sciences.

Moen, Phyllis, and Alvin L. Schorr. 1987. "Families and Social Policy." In *Handbook of Marriage and the Family,* edited by Marvin B. Sussman and Suzanne K. Steinmetz. New York: Plenum Press.

Moen, Phyllis, and Ken R. Smith. 1986. "Women at Work: Commitment and Behavior over the Life Course." *Sociological Forum* 1:450–76.

Molm, Linda. 1978. "Sex Role Attitudes and the Employment of Married Women: The Direction of Causality." *Sociological Quarterly* 19:522–33.

Moore, Kristin A., and Sandra A. Hofferth. 1979. "Women and Their Children." In *The Subtle Revolution,* edited by R. E. Smith. Washington, DC: Urban Institute.

Moorehouse, Martha J. 1991. "Linking Maternal Employment Patterns to Mother-Child Activities and Children's School Competence." *Developmental Psychology* 27:295–303.

Morgan, S. Phillip, and Linda J. Waite. 1987. "Parenthood and the Attitudes of Young Adults." *American Sociological Review* 52:1–7.

Mortimer, Jeylan T., and Donald Kuma. 1986. *Work, Family and Personality: Transition to Adulthood.* Norwood, NJ: Ablex Publishing Corporation.

Mortimer, Jeylan T., R. Hall, and R. Hill. 1978. "Husbands' Occupational Attributes as Constraints on Wives' Employment." *Sociology of Work and Occupations* 5:285–313.

Myrdal, Alva, and Viola Klein. 1956. *Women's Two Roles: Home and Work.* London: Routledge and Kegan Paul.

Nathanson, C. 1980. "Social Roles and Health Status among Women: The Significance of Employment." *Social Science and Medicine* 14:463–71.

Needleman, Ruth, and Lucretia Dewey Tanner. 1987. "Women in Unions: Current Issues." In *Working Women: Past, Present, Future*, edited by Karen Shallcross Koziara, Michael H. Moskow, and Lucretia Dewey Tanner. Washington, DC: Bureau of National Affairs.

New York State Commission on Child Care. 1986. *Talking Out About Child Care.* Albany, New York: New York State Commission on Child Care.

Nickols, Sharon Y., and E. J. Metzen. 1982. "Impact of Wife's Employment upon Husband's Housework." *Journal of Family Issues* 3:199–216.

Nine to Five, National Association of Working Women. 1986. *Working at the Margins: Part-Time and Temporary Workers in the United States.* Cleveland, OH: Nine to Five, National Association of Working Women.

Noble, Kenneth B. 1988. "Child Care: The Federal Role Grows in the '80s." *New York Times*, May 1, 4.

Nock, Steven L., and Paul W. Kingston. 1988. "Time with Children: The Impact of Couples' Work-Time Commitments." *Social Forces* 67:59–85.

Nollen, Stanley. 1982. *New Work Schedules in Practice: Managing Time in a Changing Society.* Work and Family Information Center. New York: Van Nostrand Reinhold/Work in America Series.

Northcutt, H. C. 1981. "Women, Work, and Health." *Pacific Sociological Review* 23:393–404.

Norwood, Janet L. 1985. "Jobs in the 1980's and Beyond." Address given at the Fifth International Symposium on Forecasting, Montreal, Canada, June 11.

Nye, F. Ivan. 1963. "Adjustment in the Mother: Summary and a Frame of Reference." In *The Employed Mother in America*, edited by F. Ivan Nye and Lois W. Hoffman. Chicago: Rand McNally.

————. 1974a. "Effects on Mother." Pp. 207–25 in *Working Mothers*, edited by Lois W. Hoffman and F. Ivan Nye. San Francisco: Jossey Bass.

————. 1974b. "Husband-Wife Relationship." *Working Mothers*, edited by Lois W. Hoffman and F. Ivan Nye. San Francisco: Jossey Bass.

Nye, F. Ivan, and Lois W. Hoffman, eds. 1963. *The Employed Mother in America.* Chicago: Rand McNally.

Oakley, Ann. 1974. *The Sociology of Housework.* London: Martin Robertson.

O'Connell, Martin, and David E. Bloom. 1987. *Juggling Jobs and Babies: America's Child Care Challenge*. Washington, DC: Population Reference Bureau.

Olmstead, Carney, and Suzanne Smith. 1983. *The Job Sharing Handbook*. New York: Penguin.

Opinion Research Corporation. 1987. *Work and Family Life: A National Survey*. Conducted for Better Homes and Gardens. Princeton, NJ: Opinion Research Corporation.

Oppenheimer, Valerie K. 1970. *The Female Labor Force in the United States: Demographic and Economic Factors Governing Its Growth and Changing Composition*. Berkeley: University of California Press.

———. 1977. "The Sociology of Women's Economic Role in the Family." *American Sociological Review* 42:387–405.

———. 1982. *Work and the Family: A Study in Social Demography*. New York: Academic Press.

Orden, Susan R., and Norman M. Bradburn. 1969. "Working Wives and Marital Happiness." *American Journal of Sociology* 74:391–407.

Otto, H., ed. 1970. *The Family in Search of a Future*. New York: Appleton-Century.

Owen, M., and M. Cox. 1988. "Maternal Employment and the Transition to Parenthood." In *Maternal Employment and Children's Development: Longitudinal Studies*, edited by A. E. Gottfried and A. W. Gottfried. New York: Plenum Press.

Parelius, Ann P. 1975. "Change and Stability in College Women's Orientations toward Education, Family, and Work." *Social Problems* 22:420–32.

Parsons, Talcott. 1942. "Age and Sex in the Social Structure of the United States." *American Sociological Review* 7:604–16.

Parsons, Talcott, and R. Bales. 1966. *Family, Socialization, and Interaction Process*. New York: Free Press.

Pearlin, Leonard I. 1975. "Sex Roles and Depression." Pp. 191–207 in *Life-span Developmental Psychology: Normative Life Crises*, edited by D. N. Ginsberg. New York: Academic Press.

———. 1983. "Role Strains and Personal Stress." In *Psychosocial Stress: Trends in Theory and Research*, edited by Howard B. Kaplan. New York: Academic Press.

Philliber, William W., and Dana V. Hiller. 1983. "Changes in Marriage and Wife's Career As a Result of the Relative Occupational Attainments of Spouses." *Journal of Marriage and the Family* 45:161–70.

Phillips, Deborah, Kathleen McCartney, and Sandra Scorr. 1987. "Child-care Quality and Children's Social Development." *Developmental Psychology* 23:537–43.

Piotrkowski, Chaya S., and M. H. Katz. 1982. "Indirect Socialization of Children: The Effects of Mothers' Jobs on Academic Behaviors." *Child Development* 53:1520–29.

Pleck, Joseph. 1977. "The Work-Family Role System." *Social Problems* 24:417–27.

———. 1979. "Men's Family Work: Three Perspectives and Some New Data." *Family Coordinator* 28:481–89.

———. 1983. "Husbands' Paid Work and Family Roles: Current Research Issues." In *Research on the Interweave of Social Roles*, vol. 3, *Families and Jobs*, edited by H. Z. Lopata and J. H. Pleck. Greenwich, CT: JAI Press.

———. 1985. *Working Wives, Working Husbands*. Beverly Hills, CA: Sage.

———. 1986. "Employment and Fatherhood: Issues and Innovative Policies." In *The Father's Role: Applied Perspectives*, edited by Michael E. Lamb. New York: John Wiley and Sons.

Pleck, Joseph H., M. E. Lamb, and J. A. Levine. 1985. "Facilitating Future Change in Men's Family Roles." In *Men's Changing Roles in the Family*, edited by R. A. Lewis and M. Sussman. New York: Haworth.

Pleck, Joseph H., Graham L. Staines, and Linda Lang. 1980. "Conflicts between Work and Family Life." *Monthly Labor Review* 103:29–32.

Postman, Neil. 1982. *The Disappearance of Childhood*. New York: Delacorte.

Presser, Harriet B. 1986. "Shift Work among American Women and Child Care." *Journal of Marriage and the Family* 48:551–64.

———. 1987. "Work Shifts of Full-Time Dual-Earner Couples: Patterns and Contrasts by Sex of Spouse." *Demography* 24:99–112.

———. 1988. "Shift Work and Child Care among Young Dual-Earner American Parents." *Journal of Marriage and the Family* 50:133–48.

———. 1989. "Can We Make Time for Children? The Economy, Work Schedules, and Child Care." *Demography* 26:523–54.

Presser, Harriet B., and Wendy Baldwin. 1980. "Child Care as a Constraint on Employment: Prevalence, Correlates, and Bearing on the Work and Fertility Nexus." *American Journal of Sociology* 85:1202–19.

Presser, Harriet B., and Virginia Cain. 1983. "Shift Work among Dual-Earner Couples with Children." *Science* 219:876–79.

Radloff, Lenore. 1975. "Sex Differences in Depression: The Effects of Occupation and Marital Status." *Sex Roles* 1:249–65.

Rainwater, Lee. 1974. *What Money Buys: Inequality and the Social Meaning of Income*. New York: Basic Books.

Rallings, E. M., and F. Ivan Nye. 1979. "Wife-Mother Employment, Family and Society." In *Contemporary Theories about the Family*, vol. 1, edited by Wesley R. Burr, Reuben Hill, F. Ivan Nye, and Ira L. Reiss. New York: Free Press.

Rapoport, Rhona, and Robert N. Rapoport. 1975. "The Dual Career Family: A Varient Pattern and Social Change." *Human Relations* 22:3–13.

Rapoport, Robert N., and Rhona Rapoport. 1965. "Work and Family in Contemporary Society." *American Sociological Review* 30:381–93.

———. 1976. *Dual-Career Families Reconsidered*. New York: Harper Colophon.

Repetti, Rena, Karen A. Matthews, and Ingrid Waldron. 1989. "Effects of Paid Employment on Women's Mental and Physical Health." *American Psychologist* 44:1394–401.

Reskin, Barbara F. 1988. "Bringing the Men Back In: Sex Differentiation and the Devaluation of Women's Work." *Gender & Society* 2:58–81.

———, ed. 1984. *Sex Segregation in the Workplace: Trends, Explanations, Remedies*. Washington, DC: National Academy Press.

———, and Shelley Coverman. 1985. "Sex and Race in the Determinants of Psychophysical Distress: A Reappraisal of the Sex-Role Hypothesis." *Social Forces* 63:1038–59.

———, and Heidi I. Hartmann, eds. 1986. *Women's Work, Men's Work: Sex Segregation on the Job*. Washington, DC: National Academy Press.

———, and Patricia Roos. 1990. *Job Queues, Gender Queues: Women's Inroads into Male Occupations*. Philadelphia, PA: Temple University Press.

Riley, Matilda White, and John W. Riley, Jr. 1989. "The Lives of Older People and Changing Social Roles." *Annals of the American Academy of Political and Social Science* 503:14–28.

Roberts, C., R. E. Roberts, and J. Stevenson. 1982. "Women, Work, Social Support and Psychiatric Morbidity." *Social Psychiatry* 17:167–73.

Roberts, R. E., and S. J. O'Keefe. 1981. "Sex Differences in Depression Reexamined." *Journal of Health and Social Behavior* 22:394–400.

Robinson, John P. 1977. *Changes in American's Use of Time: 1965–1975*. Cleveland, OH: Communications Research Center.

———. 1985. "Changes in Time Use: An Historical Overview." In *Time, Goods and Well-Being*, edited by F. Thomas Juster and Frank P. Stafford. Ann Arbor: University of Michigan, Institute for Social Research.

———. 1988. "Who's Doing the Housework?" *American Demographics* (December): 24–28.

Rockwell, Richard, and Glen H. Elder, Jr. 1978. "Economic Depression and Postwar Opportunity in Men's Lives: A Study of Life Patterns and Health." In *Research in Community and Health*, edited by R. G. Simmons. Greenwich, CT: JAI Press.

Rosenfeld, Rachel A. 1978. "Women's Intergenerational Occupational Mobility." *American Sociological Review* 43:36–46.

———. 1980. "Race and Sex Differences in Career Dynamics." *American Sociological Review* 45:583–609.

Rosenfield, Sarah. 1980. "Sex Differences in Depression: Do Women Have Higher Rates?" *Journal of Health and Social Behavior* 21:33–42.

————. 1989. "The Effects of Women's Employment: Personal Control and Sex Differences in Mental Health." *Journal of Health and Social Behavior* 30:77–91.

Ross, Catherine E., John Mirowsky II, and Joan Huber. 1983. "Dividing Work, Sharing Work, and In-between: Marriage Patterns and Depression." *American Sociological Review* 48:809–23.

Ross, Catherine E., John Mirowsky II, and Patricia Ulbrich. 1983. "Distress and the Traditional Female Role: A Comparison of Mexicans and Anglos." *American Journal of Sociology* 89:670–82.

Ross, H., and I. Sawhill. 1975. *Time of Transition: The Growth of Families Headed by Women*. Washington, DC: Urban Institute.

Rossi, Alice S. 1965. "Barriers to the Career Choice of Engineering, Medicine or Science among American Women." In *Women in the Scientific Professions*, edited by J. A. Mattfeld and C. G. Van Aken. Cambridge, MA: MIT Press.

————, ed. 1985. *Gender and the Life Course*. Hawthorne, NY: Aldine.

Ryan, Mary. 1975. *Womanhood in America: From Colonial Times to the Present*. New York: New Viewpoints.

Saltford, Nancy C., and Ramona K. Z. Heck. 1989. "An Overview of Employee Benefits Supportive of Families." Washington, DC: Employee Benefit Research Institute.

Sanik, Margaret Mietus, and Teresa Mauldin. 1986. "Single versus Two Parent Families: A Comparison of Mothers' Time." *Family Relations* 35:53–56.

Scanzoni, John. 1970. *Opportunity and the Family*. New York: Free Press.

————. 1978. *Sex Roles, Women's Work, and Marital Conflict*. Lexington, MA: D. C. Heath.

Scanzoni, John, and Greer Litton Fox. 1980. "Sex Roles, Family and Society: The Seventies and Beyond." *Journal of Marriage and the Family* 42:743–56.

Scarr, Sandra. 1984. *Mother Care, Other Care*. New York: Basic Books.

Schwartz, Felice N. 1989. "Management Women and the New Facts of Life." *Harvard Business Review* (January-February):65–76.

Schwartz, P. 1983. "Length of Day-Care Attendance and Attachment Behavior in Eighteen-Month-Old Infants." *Child Development* 54:1073–78.

Scott, Joan W., and Louise A. Tilly. 1975. "Women's Work and Family in Nineteenth-Century Europe." *Comparative Studies in Society and History* 17:36–64.

Select Committee on Children, Youth, and Families. 1984. *Families and Child Care: Improving the Options*. Washington, DC: U.S. Government Printing Office.

Serrin, William. 1986. "Part-Time Work New Labor Trend." *New York Times*, July 9.

Shank, Susan E. 1988. "Women and the Labor Market: The Link Grows Stronger." *Monthly Labor Review* 111:3–8.

Sharp, L., and F. Ivan Nye. 1963. "Maternal Mental Health." In *The Employed Mother in America*, edited by F. Ivan Nye and Lois W. Hoffman. Chicago: Rand McNally.

Shehan, Constance. 1984. "Wives' Work and Psychological Well-Being: An Extension of Gove's Social Role Theory of Depression." *Sex Roles* 11:881–99.

Shortlidge, Richard, Larry E. Suter, and Linda J. Waite. 1977. "Changes in Child Care Arrangements of Working Women from 1965 to 1971." *Social Science Quarterly* 58:302–11.

Sieber, Sam D. 1974. "Toward a Theory of Role Accumulation." *American Sociological Review* 39:567–78.

Simpson, Ida Harper, and Paula England. 1981. "Conjugal Work Roles and Marital Solidarity." *Journal of Family Issues* 2:180–204.

Smith-Lovin, L., and A. R. Tickamyer. 1973. "Nonrecursive Models of Labor Force Participation, Fertility Behavior and Sex Role Attitudes." *American Sociological Review* 43:541–57.

Sobol, Marion. 1963. "Commitment to Work." In *The Employed Mother in America*, edited by F. Ivan Nye and Lois W. Hoffman. Chicago: Rand McNally.

Sokoloff, Natalie. 1980. *Between Money and Love: The Dialectics of Women's Home and Market Work*. New York: Praeger.

———. 1988. "Contributions of Marxism and Feminism to the Sociology of Women and Work." In *Women Working: Theories and Facts in Perspective*, edited by Ann Helton Stromberg and Shirley Harkess. Mountain View, CA: Mayfield.

Sorensen, Annamette. 1983. "Women's Employment Patterns after Marriage." *Journal of Marriage and the Family* 45:311–21.

Sorrentino, Constance. 1990. "The Changing Family in International Perspective." *Monthly Labor Review* 113:41–58.

Spalter-Roth, Roberta, and Heidi Hartmann. 1991. U.S. Senate Testimony. "Improving Women's Status in the Work Force: The Family Issues of the Future." Hearings of the Subcommitte on Employment and Productivity, Labor and Resources.

Spitze, Glenna D. 1988. "Women's Employment and Family Relations: A Review." *Journal of Marriage and the Family* 50:595–618.

Spitze, Glenna D., and Joan Huber. 1980. "Changing Attitudes toward Women's Non-Family Roles: 1938 to 1978." *Sociology of Work and Occupations* 7:317–35.

Spitze, Glenna D., and Scott J. South. 1985. "Women's Employment, Time Expenditure, and Divorce." *Journal of Family Issues* 6:307–29.

Spitze, Glenna D., and Linda J. Waite. 1981a. "Wives' Employment: The Role of Husbands' Perceived Attitudes." *Journal of Marriage and the Family* 43:117–24.

———. 1981b. "Young Women's Preferences for Market Work: Responses to Marital Events." *Research in Population Economics* 3:147–66.

Spreitzer, Elmer, Eldon E. Snyder, and David Larson. 1975. "Age, Marital Status, and Labor Force Participation as Related to Life Satisfaction." *Sex Roles* 1:235–47.

——. 1979. "Multiple Roles and Psychological Well-Being." *Sociological Focus* 12:141–48.

Staines, Graham L., and Joseph H. Pleck. 1983. *The Impact of Work Schedules on Families.* Ann Arbor: University of Michigan, Institute for Social Research.

——. 1984. "Nonstandard Work Schedules and Family Life." *Journal of Applied Psychology* 64:515–23.

Staines, Graham L., Joseph H. Pleck, L. Shepard, and Pamela O'Connor. 1978. "Wives' Employment Status and Marital Adjustment: Yet Another Look." *Psychology of Women Quarterly* 3:90–120.

Stolzenberg, Ross M., and Linda J. Waite. 1977. "Age, Fertility Expectations and Employment Plans." *American Sociological Review* 42:210–17.

Strasser, S. 1982. *Never Done: A History of American Housework.* New York: Pantheon Books.

Strober, Myra H., and Carolyn L. Arnold. 1987. "The Dynamics of Occupational Segregation among Bank Tellers." In *Gender in the Workplace,* edited by Clair Brown and Joseph A. Pechman.

Sweet, James A. 1973. *Women in the Labor Force.* New York: Academic Press.

Tangri, S. S. 1972. "Determinants of Occupational Role Innovation among College Women." *Journal of Social Issues* 28:177–82.

Tentler, Leslie Woodcock. 1979. *Wage-Earning Women: Industrial Work and Family Life in the United States, 1900–1930.* New York: Oxford University Press.

Thoits, P. A. 1983. "Multiple Identities and Psychological Well-Being: A Reformulation and Test of the Social Isolation Hypothesis." *American Sociological Review* 48:174–87.

——. 1986. "Multiple Identities: Examining Gender and Marital Status Differences in Distress." *American Sociological Review* 51:259–72.

Thoits, Peggy, and Michael Hannan. 1979. "Income and Psychological Distress: The Impact of an Income Maintenance Experiment." *Journal of Health and Social Behavior* 20:120–38.

Thornton, A., and D. Freedman. 1979. "Changes in the Sex Role Attitudes of Women, 1962–1977: Evidence from a Panel Study." *American Sociological Review* 44:831–42.

Thornton, A., D. F. Alwin, and D. Camburn. 1983. "Causes and Consequences of Sex-Role Attitudes and Attitude Change." *American Sociological Review* 48:211–27.

Thurow, Lester. 1984. "62 Cents to the Dollar: The Earnings Gap Doesn't Go Away." *Working Mother,* October, 42.

Tilly, Louise A., and Joan W. Scott. 1978. *Women, Work, and Family.* New York: Holt, Rinehart and Winston.

Tobias, Sheila, and Lisa Anderson. 1974. "What Really Happened to Rosie the Riveter? Demobilization and the Female Labor Force 1944–47." New York: MMS Moduler Publications, Module 9.

Townsend, Allen, and Patricia Gurin. 1981. "Re-examining the Frustrated Homemaker Hypothesis: Role Fit, Personal Dissatisfaction, and Collective Discontent." *Sociology of Work and Occupations* 8:464–88.

Townsend, Bickley, and Kathleen O'Neil. 1990. "American Women Get Mad." *American Demographics* (August):26–32.

Trzcinski, Eileen. 1989. "Employers' Parental Leave Policies: Does the Labor Market Provide Parental Leave via Market Forces of Supply and Demand?" In *Parental Leave and Childcare: Setting a Research and Policy Agenda*, edited by J. Hyde. Philadelphia: Temple University Press.

———. 1991. "Separate versus Equal Treatment Approaches to Parental Leave: Theoretical Issues and Empirical Evidence." *Law and Policy*, 13: forthcoming.

U.S. Bureau of the Census. 1975a. "Daytime Care of Children." *Current Population Reports*, Series P-20, no. 298. Washington, DC: Government Printing Office.

———. 1975b. *Historical Statistics of the United States, Colonial Times to Present*. Washington, DC: U.S. Government Printing Office.

———. 1982. "Trends in Child Care Arrangements of Working Women." *Current Population Reports*, Series P-23, no. 117. Washington, DC: Government Printing Office.

———. 1983. "Child Care Arrangements of Working Mothers: June 1982." *Current Population Reports* Series P-23, no. 129. Washington, DC: Government Printing Office.

———. 1986. *Statistical Abstract of the United States*. Washington, DC: U.S. Government Printing Office.

———. 1987. "Who's Minding the Kids? Child Care Arrangements: Winter 1984–85." *Current Population Reports*. Series P-70, no. 9. Washington, DC: Government Printing Office.

———. 1989. *Statistical Abstract of the United States, 1989*. Washington, DC: U.S. Government Printing Office.

———. 1990a. "Marital Status and Living Arrangements: March 1989." *Current Population Reports* Series P-20, No. 445. Washington, DC: U.S. Government Printing Office.

———. 1990b. *Statistical Abstract of the United States*. Washington, DC: U.S. Government Printing Office.

U.S. Department of Education, National Center for Education Statistics. 1988. *Digest of Education Statistics, 1988*, CS 88–600. Washington, DC: U.S. Government Printing Office.

U.S. Departent of Labor. 1988. *Childcare: A Workforce Issue*. Report of the Secretary's Task Force. April. Washington, DC: Government Printing Office.

Vandell, Deborah L. and Mary A. Corasaniti. 1988. "The Relation between Third Graders' After-School Care and Social, Academic, and Emotional Functioning." *Child Development* 59:868–75.

———. 1990. "Child Care and the Family: Complex Contributors to Child Development." *New-Directions-for-Child-Development* 49:23–37.

Vanek, Joann. 1974. "Time Spent in Housework." *Scientific American* 231:116–20.

———. 1980. "Household Work, Wage Work and Sexual Equality." Pp. 275–92 in *Women and Household Labor*, edited by S. F. Berk. Beverly Hills: Sage.

Vaughn, B., K. Deane, and E. Waters (1985). "The Impact of Out-of-Home Care on Child-Mother Attachment Quality: Another Look at Some Enduring Questions. In *Growing Points in Attachment Theory and Research*, edited by J. Bretherton and E. Waters.

Verbrugge, Lois M. 1982. "Work Satisfaction and Physical Health." *Journal of Community Health* 7:262–83.

———. 1983. "Multiple Roles and Physical Health of Women and Men." *Journal of Health and Social Behavior* 24:16–30.

———. 1985. "Gender and Health: An Update on Hypotheses and Evidence." *Journal of Health and Social Behavior* 26:156–82.

———. 1987. "Role Burdens and Physical Health of Women and Men." In *Spouse, Parent, Worker: On Gender and Multiple Roles*, edited by Faye J. Crosby. New Haven, CT: Yale University Press.

Veroff, Joseph, Elizabeth Douvan, and Richard A. Kulka. 1981. *The Inner American: A Self Portrait from 1957 to 1976*. New York: Basic Books.

Vobejda, Barbara. 1991. "Keep Those Booties Coming: The Baby Boomerang Returns." *Washington Post National Weekly Edition*, January 28–February 3, 39.

Voydanoff, Patricia. 1988. "Work Role Characteristics, Family Structure Demands, and Work/Family Conflict." *Journal of Marriage and the Family* 50:749–61.

Voydanoff, Patricia, and Robert F. Kelly. 1984. "Determinants of Work-Related Family Problems among Employed Parents." *Journal of Marriage and the Family* 46:881–92.

Waite, Linda J. 1980. "Working Wives and the Family Cycle." *American Journal of Sociology* 86:272–94.

Waite, Linda J., and Ross Stolzenberg. 1976. "Intended Childbearing and Labor Force Participation of Young Women: Insights from Nonrecursive Models." *American Sociological Review* 41:235–52.

Waite, Linda J., Gus W. Haggstrom, and David E. Kanouse. 1985. "Changes in the Employment Activities of New Parents." *American Sociological Review* 50:263–72.

Waite, Linda, Richard L. Shortledge, Jr., and Larry E. Sutter. 1977. "Changes in Child Care Arrangements for Working Women from 1965 to 1971." *Social Quarterly* 58:302–11.

Walby, Sylvia. 1986. *Patriarchy at Work*. Minneapolis: University of Minnesota Press.

Waldman, Elizabeth. 1983. "Labor Force Statistics from a Family Perspective." *Monthly Labor Review* 106:16–20. December.

Waldron, Ingrid, and J. Jacobs. 1988. "Effects of Labor Force Participation on Women's Health: New Evidence from a Longitudinal Study." *Journal of Occupational Medicine* 30:977–83.

———. 1989. "Effects of Multiple Roles on Women's Health—Evidence for a National Longitudinal Study." *Women and Health* 15:3–19.

Waldron, Ingrid, J. Herold, D. Dunn, and R. Staum. 1982. "Reciprocal Effects of Health and Labor Force Participation among Women: Evidence from Two Longitudinal Studies." *Journal of Occupational Medicine* 24:126–32.

Walker, Kathryn E., and Margaret E. Woods. 1976. *Time Use: A Measure of Household Production of Family Goods and Services*. Washington, DC: American Home Economics Association.

Wallace, P. A. 1980. *Black Women in the Labor Force*. Cambridge, MA: MIT Press.

Wandersee, Winifred D. 1988. *On the Move: American Women in the 1970s*. Boston: Twayne.

Warr, Peter B., and G. Parry. 1982. "Paid Employment and Women's Psychological Well-Being." *Psychological Bulletin* 91(3):498–516.

Wattenberg, Ben. 1987. *The Birth Dearth*. New York: Pharos Books.

Webber, Stephen. 1985. "Testimony." *Congressional Hearing on Parental and Disability Leave*. Washington, DC, October.

Weingarten, K. 1978. "The Employment Pattern of Professional Couples and Their Distribution of Involvement in the Family." *Psychology of Women Quarterly* 3:43–52.

Weinraub, M., E. Jaeger, and L. W. Hoffman. 1988. "Predicting Infant Outcomes in Families of Employed and Non-Employed Mothers." *Early Childhood Research Quarterly* 3:361–78.

Weitzman, Lenore. 1985. *The Divorce Revolution*. New York: Free Press.

Welch, S., and A. Booth. 1977. "Employment and Health among Married Women with Children." *Sex Roles* 3:385–97.

Westinghouse Learning Corporation and Westat Research, Incorporated. 1971. *Day Care Survey—1970: Summary Report and Basic Analysis*. Washington, DC: Evaluation Division, Office of Economic Opportunity.

Wethington, Elaine. 1990. "Managing Time and Emotion: Employment and Family Role Characteristics and Health among Married Women." Paper presented at the annual meeting of the Society for the Study of Social Problems, Washington, DC, August.

Wethington, Elaine. 1992. Wives Employment and Husbands' Psychological Distress: A Reexamination. Unpublished Draft.

Wethington, Elaine, and Ronald C. Kessler. 1989. "Employment, Parenting Responsibility, and Psychological Distress: A Longitudinal Study of Married Women." *Journal of Family Issues* 10:527–46.

Wethington, Elaine, Ronald C. Kessler, and Niall Bolger. 1990. "Role Stress and Psychological Distress among Married Couples." Paper presented at the annual meeting of the American Psychological Association. Boston, August.

Whitham, Michelle, and Phyllis Moen. 1992. "Women's Employment and Life Satisfaction in the 1950s: A Test of the Role Preference Hypothesis" (unpublished draft).

Willer, Barbara. 1986. "An Investigation of the Work–Family Interface for Families with Young Children." Ph.D. diss., Cornell University.

Women's Bureau. 1946. *Women Workers in Ten War Production Areas and Their Postwar Employment Plans.* U.S. Women's Bureau Bulletin 209. Washington, DC: U.S. Department of Labor.

———. 1971. *Day Care Services: Industry's Involvement.* Washington, DC: U.S. Department of Labor.

———. 1983. *Time of Change: 1983 Handbook on Women Workers,* Bulletin 298. Washington, DC: U.S. Government Printing Office.

Woods, Margaret B. 1972. "The Unsupervised Child of the Working Woman." *Developmental Psychology* 6: 14–25.

Woods, N. F. and B. S. Hulka. 1979. "Symptom Reports and Illness Behavior among Employed Women and Housewives." *Journal of Community Health* 5:36–45.

Work and Family Life. 1987. Vol. 1.

Wright, James D. 1978. "Are Working Wives Really More Satisfied? Evidence from Several National Surveys." *Journal of Marriage and the Family* 40:301–13.

Yohalem, Alice M. 1979. *The Careers of Professional Women: Commitment and Conflict.* Montclair, NJ: Allenheld Osmun, Inc.

Zaslow, Martha J., Frank A. Pedersen, J. D. Suwalsky, and B. A. Rabinovich. 1989. "Maternal Employment and Parent-Infant Interaction at One Year." *Early Childhood Research Quarterly* 4:459–78.

Zaslow, Martha J., Frank A. Pedersen, J. D. Suwalsky, R. L. Cain, and M. Fivel. 1985. "The Early Resumption of Employment by Mothers: Implications for Parent-Infant Interaction." *Journal of Applied Developmental Psychology* 6:1–16.

INDEX

About the Author

PHYLLIS MOEN is Director of Cornell Life Course Institute and Professor of Human Development and Family Studies and of Sociology at Cornell University. Among her earlier publications are *Working Parents: Transformations in Gender Roles and Public Policies in Sweden* (1989) and numerous articles in scholarly journals.